100 GREAT WAYS TO MAKE CARDS

SHIRLEY TOOGOOD

D&C

David and Charles

A DAVID & CHARLES BOOK
Copyright © David & Charles Limited 2007

David & Charles is an F+W Publications Inc. company
4700 East Galbraith Road, Cincinnati, OH 45236

First published in the UK in 2007
Reprinted in 2007 (3 times)
Text and project designs copyright © Shirley Toogood 2007
Shirley Toogood has asserted her right to be identified
as author of this work in accordance with the
Copyright, Designs and Patents Act, 1988.

A catalogue record for this book is available from the
British Library.

ISBN-13: 978-0-7153-2591-9 hardback
ISBN-10: 0-7153-2591-4 hardback
ISBN-13: 978-0-7153-2308-3 paperback
ISBN-10: 0-7153-2308-3 paperback

Printed in China by SNP Leefung
for David & Charles
Brunel House   Newton Abbot   Devon

Executive Editor Cheryl Brown
Editor Jennifer Proverbs
Desk Editor Bethany Dymond
Senior Designer Charly Bailey
Production Controller Kelly Smith

Visit our website at www.davidandcharles.co.uk

David & Charles books are available from all good
bookshops; alternatively you can contact our
Orderline on 0870 9908222 or write to us at FREEPOST
EX2 110, D&C Direct, Newton Abbot, TQ12 4ZZ (no
stamp required UK only); US customers call 800-289-
0963 and Canadian customers call 800-840-5220.

*The author and publisher have made every effort to
ensure that all the instructions in the book are accurate
and safe, and therefore cannot accept liability for any
resulting injury, damage or loss to persons or property,
however it may arise.*

*Names of manufacturers, paper ranges and other
products are provided for the information of readers, with
no intention to infringe copyright or trademarks.*

CONTENTS

INTRODUCTION 4
Basic Tool Kit 5

RUBBER STAMPS 6
1 Butterfly Dream
2 For the Love of Flowers
3 Eggcellent Easter
4 Shadow Play

HEAT EMBOSSING 10
5 Putting on the Glitz
6 Rocket Racer
7 Bobbing Balloons
8 Gone Fishing

PAPER EMBOSSING 14
9 Baby Charm
10 Harlequin
11 Old-world Charm
12 Dream Cake

TAGS 18
13 Fond Farewell
14 Into the Blue
15 Silver Anniversary
16 Tiny Tags for Big News

MULBERRY PAPER 22
17 Hearts and Flowers
18 Flowers of the Field
19 Star of Wonder
20 In the Frame

BEADS 26
21 Career Ladder
22 From the Heart
23 Little Brown Mouse
24 Parcel Post

PAINTS, CRAYONS AND PENCILS 30
25 Super Skater
26 Mists of Time
27 Soft and Simple
28 Flower Power

WIRE 34
29 Animal Magic
30 Absolutely Charming
31 Star Player
32 Proud Peacock

RIBBON 38
33 Home Patch
34 Woven Cross
35 Lovely in Lavender
36 Jingle Bells

PHOTOGRAPHS 42
37 Going for Gold
38 Mosaic Masterpiece
39 Christmas Greetings
40 Garden Harvest

RUB-ONS 46
41 Magic Circles
42 Say It With Numbers
43 Perfect Party
44 Fairy Ring

PUNCHES 50
45 Swirling Leaves
46 Flower Dimensions
47 Two Hearts as One
48 All Hands on Deck

Threads and Fibres   54
49 Sew Easy
50 Haunting Halloween
51 Baby Feet
52 Simple Spirelli

Vellum   58
53 Ocean Waves
54 Flower Fancy
55 Love Letter
56 Sheer Abstract

Confetti   62
57 Have a Heart
58 Baby Ted
59 Tree Star
60 Turkey Trot

Collage   66
61 Snow Business
62 Stars & Stripes
63 No Place Like Home
64 Out of Africa

Eyelets and Brads   70
65 Baby Fashion
66 Chinese Fortune
67 Lovely Luggage
68 Ring Out the Romance

Die Cuts   74
69 Ghostly Glow
70 Pop-up Flowers
71 Small Packages
72 Starry, Starry Night

Parchment Craft and Paper Pricking   78
73 Easter Elegance
74 Golden Koi
75 Bunny for Baby
76 Christmas in the Round

Teabag Folding   82
77 'Tis the Season
78 Dancing Butterflies
79 Stamped Sensation
80 Let's Fly a Kite

Stickers and Peel-Offs   86
81 Crocus for Mother
82 Luck of the Irish
83 Dragonfly Days
84 Birthday Band

Polymer Clay   90
85 Scroll of Honour
86 On the Road
87 Ruby Wedding
88 Three Little Ducks

Stencils   94
89 From Leaf to Petal
90 Here Comes the Sun
91 Birthday Bunch
92 Snow Romance

Metal   98
93 Lingering Love
94 Lucky Horseshoes
95 Potty About Plants
96 Key to the Door

Quilling   102
97 King of the Jungle
98 Spot the Flowers
99 Around and Around
100 Fashionista's Favourite

Templates   106
Suppliers and Stockists   111
Acknowledgments   112
Index   112

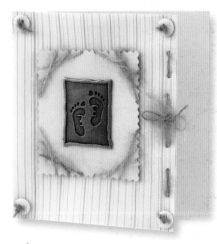

INTRODUCTION

Card making is a wonderfully creative craft for people of all ages and abilities. Using stickers, rub-ons, punched shapes, papers, ribbons and more you can produce wonderful cards quickly and easily, simply by copying the designs in this book. With 25 different techniques and 100 super cards to choose from there's something for every taste and occasion.

With the beginner and intermediate card maker in mind, this book contains a range of projects explained in simple stages with photographic illustrations to help you every step of the way, and you'll even find full-size templates for the more complex shapes required. Simple motifs provide a quick visual reference to the suggested use of each card (see the key, right) and every project has a handy tip, so you'll soon know all the shortcuts.

OCCASION KEY

Celebrations through the year

Happy birthday

Children's birthday celebrations

Celebrating baby

Wish them luck

Wonderful weddings

Romance and anniversaries

Greetings for men

Greetings for all

Christmas wishes

Bon voyage

Celebrating achievements

CARD BLANKS

The basis for nearly every project in this book is a card blank, available from card making suppliers (see page 111). These come in a number of types, sizes, colours, weights and finishes. Choose from neutral shades, pastels and bright colours, as well as matt, metallic and pearl finishes or opt for a luxurious material such as watercolour and handmade papers. Envelopes are available to fit most sizes.

Standard aperture cards have a window on the front that can be round, oval, square, rectangular or a speciality shape, like a Christmas tree.

Double-fold aperture cards have three panels so that one panel acts as a backing for the aperture. Ideal for placing pictures, embroidery, mini quilts or other items to hide any raw or rough edges.

Single-fold cards are inexpensive, versatile card blanks and can be used as the base for any design.

Embossed cards often have an embossed border, sometimes with foil embellishment. Simply add your design inside the frame. You can also add your own embossing to a single-fold card (see page 14).

Decorative-edge cards are single-fold cards with a decorative edge. Alternatively, cut your own decorative edges using scissors or cutters.

CARD SHAPES AND SIZES

These are variable and the range is ever increasing. Popular sizes include the following, though of course you can always make a custom size by trimming a larger blank or by making your own card blank from coloured card:

Rectangular: 56 x 89mm (2¼ x 3½in), 88 x 114mm (3½ x 4½in), 104 x 152mm (4 x 6in or A6), 114 x 178mm (4½ x 7in) and 150 x 203mm (6 x 8in or A5).

Tall: 69 x 184mm (2¾ x 7¼in) and 100 x 210mm (4 x 8¼in).

Square: 100 x 100mm (4 x 4in) and 144 x 144mm (5¾ x 5¾in).

MAKING YOUR OWN CARD

If you wish to use unusual paper for the card blank or can't find the size you want in the right colour, you can easily make your own card blank as follows, though do work to the sizes listed previously to ensure you can buy a matching envelope.

1 Using a sharp knife and ruler or trimmer, cut your card twice the required width by the required height. Measure across the top and bottom of the card and lightly mark the centre with pencil. Place a ruler between the marks and score down the edge with a stylus or bone folder.

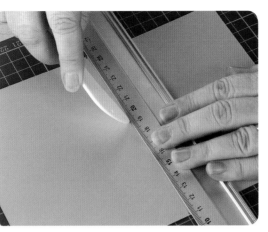

2 Fold the card along the scored line. For a professional finish smooth along the fold with a bone folder or the back of a clean plastic ruler. If desired, trim the edges with decorative-edge scissors.

CARD-MAKER'S BASIC TOOL KIT

There is a core of basic equipment you'll need for making the projects in this book and elsewhere, much of which you'll already have. It's listed here for your convenience. If you need to buy any items, buy the best you can afford to ensure they give good service.

Bone folder – for professional-looking folds.

Craft knife – a sharp blade is essential so pick a style that makes it easy for you to replace the blade.

Cutting mat – a self-healing mat is best.

Embossing or ball tool – used for scoring, embossing, transferring rub-ons and positioning small items.

Eraser – keep it clean and use a putty rubber to remove stray glue.

Glues – choose glue stick and basic white craft glue (PVA) plus specialist glues for adding charms and other non-paper items.

Glue dots – these are easy to use and give a very strong bond.

Metal non-slip ruler – preferably one with a finger guard.

Pencil – I like propelling pencils for a constant sharp point.

Scissors – ideally get a standard pair of paper scissors, a very small pair for cutting intricate shapes and a non-stick pair for tacky items.

Sticky foam pads – these are used to raise part of the card from the surface, giving it life and a three-dimensional look.

Vellum adhesives – there are several on the market but for small areas, glue stick applied very thinly and left to dry slightly works quite well, or you can use eyelets or brads instead. For larger areas, spray mount is easier to use than glues and tapes.

Watercolour paintbrush – to apply paint and manipulate small items.

When applying glue to small shapes work on scrap paper so you can take the glue right up to the edges without worrying about making a mess.

The following are invaluable additions to your tool kit:

Cocktail sticks – these have hundreds of uses from sticking tiny items and removing excess glue to making holes.

Masking tape – this low-tack tape is very useful for holding stencils in place or for masking as it can be removed easily. Use with care – it is not suitable for paper with a very soft surface.

Rotary cutter, trimmer or guillotine – one of your bigger investments, a cutter makes short work of cutting rectangles and squares.

Tweezers – not essential but handy for picking up small items.

Double-sided tape – excellent for sticking ribbons and edgings; the wider versions are great for sticking backing papers.

Sheet adhesives, such as Xyron – these are very useful for sticking tiny, awkward shapes, covering them with adhesive without mess.

RUBBER STAMPS

Using rubber stamps we can all produce beautiful, sharp images without the need to draw. The pictures created can be coloured in, cut up, layered, given sparkle with glitter or over-stamped. Work on any relatively smooth paper and use waterproof ink for stamping if you want to colour in an image afterwards without smudging the lines.

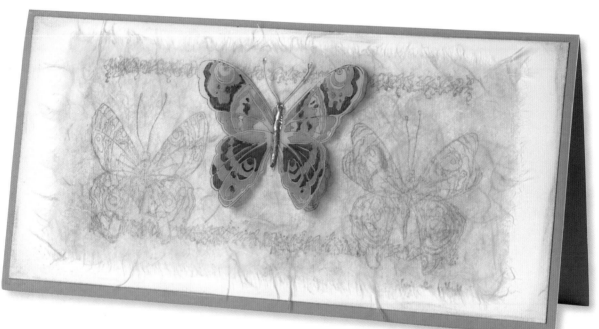

1 BUTTERFLY DREAM

23 **Apply chalk to images stamped in watermark ink for a lovely soft effect.** Here the technique is used to create a soft background for a three-dimensional butterfly with vellum wings. This makes a magical Mother's Day card.

■ Turquoise card blank 100 x 210mm (4 x 8¼in) ■ Pale turquoise mulberry paper ■ White card ■ Scrap of vellum ■ Butterfly stamp with three butterflies about 17cm (16¾in) across ■ Watermark and purple inkpads ■ Pastel chalks in mauve, blue and turquoise and chalk applicator ■ Metallic rub-on wax in blue ■ Felt-tip or gel pens in pink and turquoise ■ Tube of silver three-dimensional paint

1 Use water and a small brush to outline a rectangle 19 x 8cm (7½ x 3in) on the mulberry paper. Tear along the wet lines to remove the rectangle, as shown.

2 Using the watermark ink, stamp the butterfly design in the middle of the mulberry paper rectangle. If the stamp is unavailable, stamp three individual butterflies in roughly the same positions.

3 Dust the stamped images with chalks, using blocks of colour and covering the whole area so that the inked lines pick up the chalk colours, as shown. Overlap different colours in places.

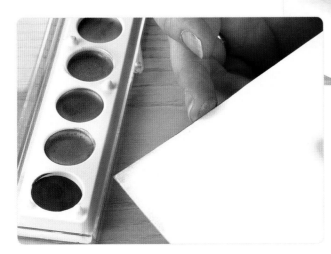

4 Cut a rectangle of white card slightly smaller than the card blank. Stick your finger in blue rub-on metallic wax and rub it along the edges of the card. Repeat to colour all the edges.

5 When the wax is dry, stick the mulberry paper centrally on the white card.

Stamp on a flat surface with a slight give. Placing a magazine or something similar beneath your paper will be better than stamping directly on to a hard work surface.

6 Stamp one butterfly in purple on the vellum, as shown.

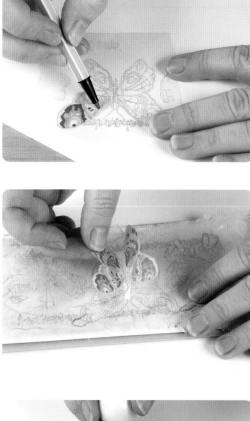

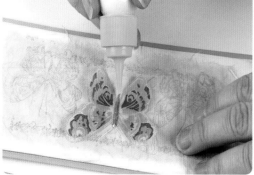

Stamp an image in two or more colours for greater impact. It's fun and fashionable. Here the design is stamped on to white card that is applied to the card with foam pads to raise it off the surface. This is perfect as a pretty birthday card.

■ White card blank 100 x 100mm (4 x 4in) ■ Pink spotted paper 90 x 90mm (3½ x 3½in) ■ White card ■ Diamond background stamp and small flower stamp ■ Flower on stem stamp about 8cm (3in) high ■ Deep pink and green inkpads ■ Pink sheer sparkly ribbon ■ Pink craft foam heart shape ■ Rounded corner punch ■ Heat gun

7 Allow the stamped image to dry then colour it in with pink and turquoise felt-tips or gel pens, as shown (top). Next cut out the butterfly, fold it in half and stick the fold over the central butterfly on the mulberry paper so the wings are slightly raised (centre). Finally, use three-dimensional paint to create a body on top of the vellum butterfly (bottom), and add dots to the upper ends of the antennae. Mount the decorative panel centrally on the front of the card blank to finish.

1 Stamp a background design in deep pink on the pink spotted paper. Now use the punch to round off the corners of the pink paper. Press the edges of the paper on the pink inkpad to colour them. When the ink is dry, stick the pink paper to the front of the white card blank and ink its edges in the same way.

2 Ink the flower stamp in green and pink and stamp on to white card. Trim the card, round off the corners and ink up the edges as before. Wrap pink ribbon around the card and glue the ends to the back. Stick the image to the card with foam pads.

3 Heat the pink foam heart with a heat gun (on a heat-proof surface) until it softens and then press the small flower stamp into it to de-boss an image. Leave to cool then stick on the card.

If you find it fiddly stamping in more than one colour, look out for stamp pens. These work like felt-tips – just colour in the design on the stamp then stamp the image. Work quickly – these pens dry fast.

3 EGGCELLENT EASTER

Apply a stamped motif repeatedly for a modern designer look. Use watercolours or felt-tips to add colour to the simple but stylish patterns on each one.

1 Stamp six eggs with black ink on white card and decorate them with watercolour paints or felt-tips.

2 Use a pencil to mark out six 4.5cm (1¾in) squares, equally spaced, on the front of the card. Cut 4.5cm (1¾in) squares of foam and use these to stamp six coloured squares on the card (see the tip below).

3 Leave to dry then rub out the pencil marks and draw wavy lines along the edges of the squares with gold pen. Cut out the stamped eggs and fix them in the centres of the squares using sticky foam pads.

When using foam to make a stamp, stick it to a cork or piece of dowel to act as a handle.

■ Lemon yellow card blank 104 x 152mm (4 x 6in) ■ White card or smooth watercolour paper ■ Small sheet of craft foam in any colour ■ Small egg stamp about 3cm (1¼in) high ■ Waterproof black inkpad ■ Mauve, green, orange, blue, yellow and pink inkpads ■ Watercolour paints or felt-tip pens in mauve, green, orange, blue, yellow and pink ■ Gold gel pen

4 SHADOW PLAY

Stamp on to acetate so your motifs seem to float over the background. Here the same stamped motifs are applied to the acetate and to the paper underneath so the top layer stands out and the lower layer fades like a shadow into the background. This makes a striking graduation card.

1 Stamp four mortarboards at angles down the acetate using dark blue ink (see the tip below right).

2 Stamp five green and five pale blue mortarboards on the front of the turquoise card blank, alternating the colours and overlapping the motifs for a random look.

3 Attach the stamped acetate rectangle to the front of the card with an eyelet in each corner (see pages 70–71).

4 To frame the image nicely cut very narrow strips of marbled paper and stick these close to each edge of the card around the acetate as a stylish border.

■ Turquoise card blank 69 x 184mm (2¾ x 7¼in) ■ Acetate rectangle 5 x 16.5cm (2 x 6½in) ■ Marbled paper ■ Mortarboard stamp ■ Inkpads in dark blue, pale blue and green suitable for shiny surfaces such as StazOn solvent-based ink or BIP Brilliance Archive Pads ■ Dark blue star eyelets ■ Eyelet setting tools

Stamps can easily slip on acetate. Practise a few times before you work on your card and press quite lightly to reduce the chance of slipping.

Heat Embossing

Give your stamped images extra dimension by embossing them. All you have to do is add embossing powder to the wet ink and heat it to melt it with a specialist heat tool. Powders are available in numerous gorgeous colours, or to give clear glossy, glittery or metallic finishes. You needn't only use them on stamped images – metal or card shapes can be embossed as well.

5 Putting on the Glitz

Add glitter to melted embossing powder for stamped images with added glamour. For denser coverage, apply glitter to areas of PVA glue. This idea is great for a teenage girl, using flowers, hearts and clothing stamps alongside a girl motif.

- Shocking pink card rectangle 30 x 15cm (12 x 6in)
- White card rectangle 15 x 10cm (6 x 4in)
- Scraps of pink and mauve card
- Rubber stamps in a variety of designs including a girl
- Inkpads in pink and mauve plus embossing ink
- Glossy clear and black embossing powders
- Pink and silver glitters ■ PVA glue ■ Heat tool
- Rounded corner punch

1 Cut out a selection of pink and mauve card circles 1–3.5cm (½–1½in) in diameter – punches make this easy, if you have some. Stamp a motif in the centre of one using coloured ink. Before the ink dries, shake clear embossing powder over the stamped image and shake off the surplus.

2 Heat the powder with the heat tool until it melts. While it is still melted, sprinkle a small pinch of pink or silver glitter over it (not so much that it covers the embossing completely) shake off the excess and allow the card to cool.

3 Dab PVA glue around the edge of the card circle and shake glitter over it. This gives a denser glitter than the previous method. Allow the glue to dry. Repeat with the other circles.

Use tweezers to hold small pieces of card when embossing or adding glue or glitter.

4 Stamp the girl motif on to the white card rectangle using embossing ink. Cover it with black embossing powder, tip off the excess and heat until it melts. Stamp and emboss pink stars around the girl using the same method as before. Working on one side at a time, edge the white card with pink ink and emboss, adding glitter for sparkle.

5 Score a line 7cm (2¾in) from each edge of the pink card rectangle and fold in each side. Press the folds with a bone folder. Stick the white card centrally on top, as shown.

6 Use the corner punch to shape the card edges, then apply embossing ink and clear embossing powder. Melt the powder and add pinches of glitter. Stick the embossed circles to the card front, as shown, for a perfect finish.

6 ROCKET RACER

Don't reserve embossing for the main motifs, use it to make **stunning backgrounds too**. In this super birthday card, the rocket flies over an embossed background of glittering planets.

1 Stamp the space stamp on to blue card and sprinkle the ink with embossing powder. Heat the powder with the heat tool until it melts.

2 Ink the rocket stamp with embossing ink and stamp it on to the silver card. Emboss as before. When dry colour the flames with red felt-tip. Cut out the rocket.

3 Cut a 3cm (1¼in) circle of acetate. Make a small hole in the centre and fix the acetate to the blue card using the brass brad. Stick the rocket on to the acetate circle so that it will rotate.

4 Trim the blue card and stick it to the yellow card blank with foam pads.

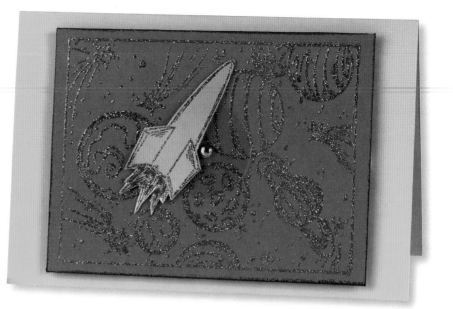

■ Yellow card blank 104 x 152mm (4 x 6in) ■ Blue card and silver card ■ Acetate sheet ■ Rocket and space stamps ■ Orange, green and yellow inkpads and an embossing inkpad ■ Sparkling embossing powder ■ Heat tool ■ Red felt-tip pen ■ Brass brad

Always clean the stamp pads after use.

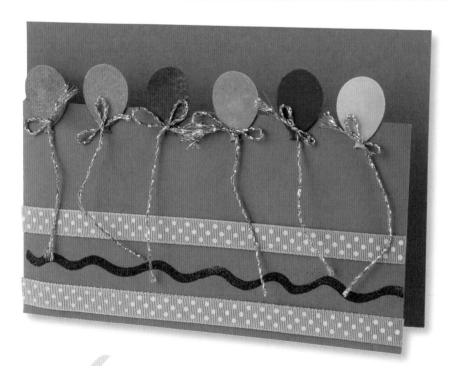

7 BOBBING BALLOONS

Cover punched shapes with clear embossing powder and heat for **a glossy finish**. Use the punched shapes to embellish birthday cards with ease.

1 Punch balloon shapes from each colour of card. Press each shape on to the embossing inkpad, coat in clear embossing powder and emboss.

2 Cut a 3 x 15cm (1¼ x 6in) strip from the top front of the card and stick the balloons along the edge as in the photograph, left.

3 Using the embossing pen, draw a wavy line across the card 2cm (1in) from the bottom. Emboss with blue gloss embossing powder. Add ribbon trims then add bows to the balloons in metallic thread.

To prevent embossing powder sticking to the card where you don't want it to, wipe the card with an anti-static pad or dust with talcum powder and wipe off.

■ Blue card blank 104 x 152mm (4 x 6in) ■ Scraps of brightly coloured card in blue, orange, yellow, red, bright green and purple ■ Small balloon punch ■ Embossing inkpad ■ Embossing pen ■ Clear and blue gloss embossing powders ■ Pale blue spotted ribbon ■ Blue metallic embroidery thread (floss) ■ Heat tool

8 GONE FISHING

Expand the possibilities by embossing freehand drawings using an embossing pen and powders. Your motifs don't have to be complex to work well – these fish are easy to draw but have real impact, making this the ideal card for a keen fisherman.

1 Draw a simple fish on gold paper in pencil. When you are happy with the design, draw over the pencil with an embossing pen, as shown.

2 Sprinkle gold embossing powder over the pen lines and shake off the excess.

3 Heat to emboss the design. Repeat to emboss several fish on each gold paper. Cut out your fish.

4 Draw a vertical wavy line on the card front with the embossing pen and emboss with the green powder to look like seaweed. Repeat to add more strands, working each one individually.

5 Stick the fish in position on the card. Draw bubbles and emboss them with clear embossing powder.

6 Finally, emboss the edges of the card as in step 4 for a neat finish, if desired.

■ Green card blank 104 x 152mm (6 x 4in) ■ Gold paper in two shades ■ Embossing pen ■ Clear, gold and glittery green embossing powders ■ Heat tool

When using embossing powder, always place a large sheet of paper under the piece you are working on. When you are finished, brush the excess powder on to the paper so you can tip it back into its container and use it later.

PAPER EMBOSSING

Paper embossing is an easy technique, requiring very few tools for stunning results. Use it to create a raised design on paper or card for a professional finish and a chic or pretty look. Embossing combines well with other paper-craft techniques such as punching, using stickers or paints, and can be coloured or sanded for different effects.

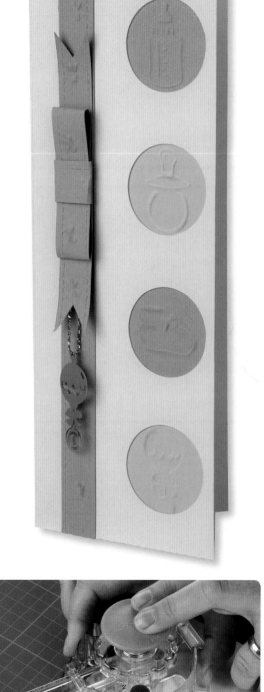

9 BABY CHARM

Use tiny embossed motifs for a modern card to celebrate the birth of a baby. Embossed motifs placed behind circular apertures add delightful embellishment to this card, which is completed with an embossed paper ribbon bow. A single stencil, hung from the paper bow like a charm, is the perfect final touch.

- Pale yellow card blank 69 x 184mm (2¾ x 7¼in)
- Pastel green and mauve paper or thin card
- Scrap of white card
- Four metal embossing stencils with baby designs less than 2.5cm (1in) tall and wide
- Embossing tool
- Lightbox
- Circle cutter or circular craft punches approximately 2.5cm (1in) and 3.5cm (1½in) across
- Perforator
- Gold thread

Rub your embossing tool on a clear wax candle to help it glide smoothly over the paper. This is especially helpful on rough papers. Alternatively, rub some waxed paper over your embossing paper for the same smooth results.

1 Cut four 2.5cm (1in) diameter circles down the right-hand edge of the card blank, marking the positions with pencil first to ensure that they are evenly spaced.

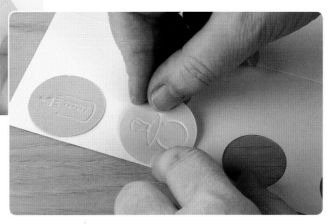

2 Place a stencil on your lightbox and the mauve paper right side down on top. Switch on the lightbox so you can see the stencil underneath the paper and press the embossing tool over the top, pushing the paper into it. Repeat to emboss another design on mauve paper and two on green paper.

3 Cut out the stencilled motifs so they are centred in circles that will fit behind the card apertures. Stick them in place, facing forwards. To cover the circle backs, cut a piece of white card slightly smaller than the front of the card and stick this inside the card.

4 Cut 1cm ($^3/_8$in) strips of mauve paper and perforate lines close to the edges, running the perforator against a ruler, as shown.

5 Pick out a small motif from one of the stencils – a bow or heart is ideal – and emboss the pattern at regular intervals along the strips of paper for further embellishment.

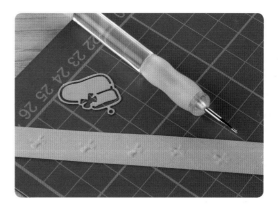

6 Stick one long strip of mauve paper down the left-hand side of the card, trimmed to size.

7 Trim a mauve strip to about 9cm (3½in) long and cut V-shaped notches in the ends. Cut another strip and bend the ends under to look like a ribbon bow. Now cut a short strip to wrap around the folded piece, creating the knot in the centre, and stick it on the notched strip, as shown. Glue the bow to the mauve strip on the card then hang a stencil from the bow using gold thread to finish.

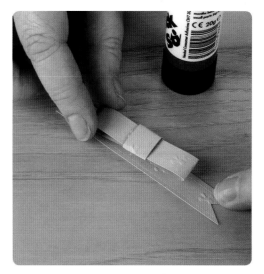

10 HARLEQUIN

Use embossing to soften a geometrical design. Vibrant, coordinating papers create a striking effect here, subtly embellished with embossed horseshoes and other good-luck motifs.

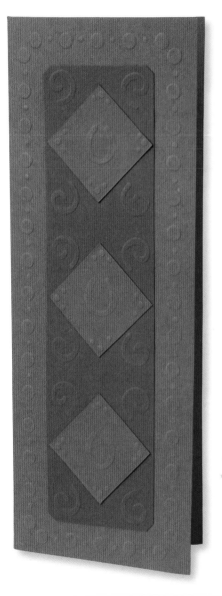

- 69 x 184mm (2¾ x 7¼in) pink card blank
- Purple card 16 x 4cm (6¼ x 1½in)
- Pink card scraps
- Horseshoe, swirl, dots and circle embossing stencils
- Embossing tool

Use a corner punch to round off the corners of paper or card neatly and easily.

1 Mark three 2.5cm (1in) squares in pencil on some pink card and emboss a motif diagonally in the centre of each one. Add three embossed dots in each corner then cut out the squares.

2 Stick the three squares down the centre of the purple card as diamonds and emboss further motifs around them. Trim the corners of the purple card to curves.

3 Emboss a pattern around the edges of your card blank and stick your purple card centrally on top.

11 OLD-WORLD CHARM

Sand down an embossed image for an antique themed birthday card. Capture the vintage look by mixing traditional patterns with elegant embossing and trimmings. Sanding and tinting give the card a lovely aged finish.

- White card blank 100mm (4in) square ■ White-cored blue card 10cm (4in) square ■ Floral paper 9cm (3½in) square ■ Decorative tag stencil ■ Embossing tool ■ Brown inkpad ■ Trimmings such as silk flowers, buttons, ribbon and fibres ■ Sandpaper or emery board ■ Decorative corner punch

1 Cut out and emboss a tag on white-cored blue card. Ink the edges of the tag using a brown inkpad. Rub sandpaper or an emery board gently over the surface of the embossed design. Decorate the tag with silk flowers and buttons, tying ribbon and fibres into the buttons.

2 Punch each corner of the floral square with a decorative corner punch. Ink the edges of the paper as before. Stick the blue card to the front of the white card blank.

3 Stick the floral paper centrally on to the front of the card then stick the tag in the centre at a slight angle, using foam pads to raise it off the surface.

To prevent your stencil from slipping out of place while you are embossing, stick it to the paper with low-tack adhesive tape.

12 DREAM CAKE

For a charming wedding card, layer your design for added dimension and highlight the embossing with coloured chalk. Emboss a design several times, cut it out to create layers, then use foam pads to raise these off the surface.

Wipe your stencil carefully with a soft cloth after chalking through it to avoid transferring chalk anywhere else.

1 Emboss the wedding cake design (see below) on to cream card. Before removing the stencil, dab coloured chalk on the flowers and decorations, using an up and down motion to avoid the coloured chalk spreading beyond the embossed area.

2 Repeat step 1 on the same type of card for the bottom two cake layers, then the bottom layer only – you should now have three embossed images.

3 Trim the first complete design to a rectangle 7.5 x 10cm (3 x 4in) then cut round the second-largest design and stick it over the corresponding section of the whole cake with foam pads. Trim around the remaining design and add this, again fixing it on with foam pads.

4 Cut a piece of gold paper slightly larger than the design and mat the whole cake on to this. Now mat it on to pink paper, this time allowing a wider border. Finally mat on to gold paper, allowing the same narrow boarder as on the first gold mat.

5 Stick the gems in the corners of the cream layer. Emboss and chalk flower patterns along the bottom of the cream card blank then stick the layered motif centrally above them.

■ Cream card blank 104 x 152mm (4 x 6in) ■ Cream card ■ Wedding cake and flower embossing stencils ■ Embossing tool (right) ■ Gold paper ■ Pink paper ■ Coloured chalks ■ Heart-shaped gems

If you cannot find a stencil similar to this one (right), emboss rings or bells on to the card to continue the wedding theme.

TAGS

Tags are so much more than mere labels. Used creatively they can be popped into pockets, hung loose from ribbon or fibre ties, or even used to make entire cards. They draw attention to whatever is on them, making them ideal for that special photo or embellishment, and because you have both sides to play with they provide twice the fun when it comes to adding the decorations.

13 FOND FAREWELL

■ Two sheets of A4 cream card ■ Patterned papers for the panels ■ Scrap card for the templates ■ Green inkpad ■ Photographs, ribbons, card scraps, buttons and other embellishments of your choice

Make an accordion-style tag-shaped card to maximize space for greetings.

When a group of people want to sign a card, perhaps for a colleague who is retiring or a friend who is going abroad, you need something that has plenty of space for photos, mementoes and warm wishes. This card is simple to cut and fold and can be decorated to suit the recipient or occasion.

1 Cut a 15 x 9cm (6 x 3½in) piece of scrap card. With a pencil, measure and mark 2.5cm (1in) down from the top of each long edge and the same measurement across the top. Draw a line across each corner between the marks and cut along the lines to create a tag template.

2 Starting at one edge of the cream card, draw round the template to mark three tag shapes side by side and touching. Use the edge of the card as the side of the first tag. Cut out your three-tag shape.

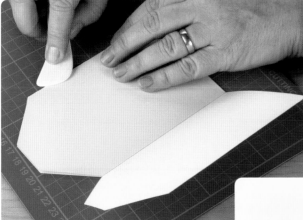

3 Score and fold down the lines where the tags meet, making the folds in opposite directions to create the accordion shape, as shown left. Using the template again, draw the tag shape six times on the back of your patterned papers. Cut each tag out individually just inside the drawn lines to create panels.

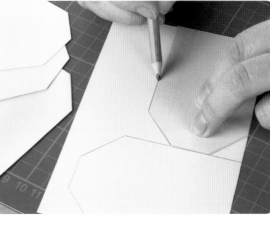

4 Cut a 9 x 6cm (3½ x 2½in) rectangle from scrap card. Measure 2cm (¾in) in each direction from the top two corners as in step 1, draw the diagonal lines and cut along them to create a tag shape. Use this template to cut five cream tags. Ink the edges of the tags with green ink.

5 Stick the decorative papers centrally on to each page – front and back – then centre a small cream tag on top and stick in place on all but the front page.

6 Decorate your card with photos, ribbons and other decorations, keeping a photograph of the recipient to go on the front. Below are some ideas.

Keep your tag templates in a file – you never know when you might want them again.

Use ribbons, buttons and other decorations to draw the eye.

Add photos and embellishments at the top so there is plenty of space for greetings, and remember that you can use both sides of the card.

Add embellishments that relate to the hobbies of the recipient.

Make a mini tag to use as an embellishment.

14 INTO THE BLUE

Use mini tags on a larger tag to spell out your greeting. This tag sits inside a pocket on the card, which has a window so your message is revealed. Wavy lines and sponged white clouds suggest fair sailing weather, but you can change the decorations and the message to adapt this card to any occasion.

- A4 sheets of card in turquoise, pale green and cream
- White acrylic paint and small natural sponge ■ Pale blue adhesive tape or blue gel pen ■ Mini alphabet tags
- Sheer green ribbon ■ Eyelet and eyelet setter tools

Instead of tying ribbon or fibre through a hole in the tag, use a decorative brad to attach it to the card.

1 Cut the turquoise card into a 12.5 x 30cm (5 x 12in) rectangle and an 8.5 x 30cm (3½ x 12in) rectangle. Cut the smaller rectangle in half to make two pieces 8.5 x 15cm (3½ x 6in). Use one piece to make the tag. With a short edge of the tag piece at the top, measure 2.5cm (1in) from the corners along the top and 4cm (1½in) down each long side. Cut between adjacent marks to create a tab shape as in step 1 on page 18.

2 Use white acrylic paint to sponge clouds on the top half of the tag, dabbing it and swirling it around a little. Make wavy lines over the bottom of the tab using pale blue adhesive flexible tape or blue gel pen. If you have used tape, rub over it with your thumb or a bone folder to ensure it is well stuck down.

3 Cut a 5 x 7.5cm (2 x 3in) rectangle of green card and a slightly smaller rectangle of cream card. Stick the cream card centrally on the green card and add your greeting spelt with mini alphabet tags.

4 Score and fold 12cm (4½in) from one end of the large piece of turquoise card. Cut a 7 x 4cm (2¾ x 1½in) aperture 1cm (³/₈in) from the end of the short part of the card.

5 Cut 1.5cm (½in) from each side of the longer half of the card. Score and fold in the resulting 1.5cm (½in) flap either side of the short end, then fold the two halves of the card together and stick the flaps to the longer half to make a pocket. Sponge clouds on to the pocket as before.

6 Stick the card with the greeting on the tag, positioning it so that it shows through the aperture in the pocket, then fit an eyelet at the top of the tag and tie green ribbon into it. Finally, pop the tag into the pocket.

15 SILVER ANNIVERSARY

Create a very special tag as a unique card or to accompany a gift. Blue, white and silver paper, ribbon, beads and charms combine for a glittery and romantic tag that will be cherished for years. Change the colours to suit a different anniversary, for a wedding or even for Christmas.

- Pale blue card ■ Fancy vellum ■ Silver braid ■ Pale blue and silver-embellished ribbon ■ Charm plaque ■ Beads, fabric flowers and other embellishments ■ Rounded corner punch (optional)

Write your greeting on a small piece of white paper and stick this on the back of your tag. Don't try to write directly on the back of the tag or you may damage the decorations.

1 Cut a 15 x 9cm (6 x 3½in) rectangle of pale blue card. Mark 2.5cm (1in) in each direction from the top corners, and cut across the corners between marks to make a tag as in step 1 on page 18.

2 Round off each angle, including the bottom corners with a punch or using a circular object as a template.

3 Tear fancy vellum to fit the centre of the tag and stick it in place with random dots of glue that can be covered by decorations.

4 Stick silver braid around the outside edge of the tag and a strip of silver-embellished ribbon across the card near the lower edge.

5 Fix a charm plaque in the centre of the vellum then stick beads randomly around it. Add further embellishments, such as flower beads and fabric flowers along the ribbon.

6 To finish, fix ribbon to the top of the tag and cover the end with another embellishment, such as a fabric flower.

---

1 Cut a 69 x 184mm (2¾ x 7¼in) piece of decorative paper or card and stick it to the card blank.

2 Cut five 2.5cm (1in) diameter circles of plain card. Fix one eyelet near the edge of each circle. Decorate with your chosen embellishments, letters or words.

3 Stick a piece of ribbon along the card 1.5cm (½in) from the fold. Loop each tag on a 4cm (1½in) length of ribbon and stick the ends to the ribbon on the card so that the tags hang down.

4 Make small bows of ribbon and stick them at the tops of the loops for a final flourish.

16 TINY TAGS FOR BIG NEWS

Use small tags to spell out a greeting or display thematic motifs. You can tie lots of them to a card to announce a baby's birth or for any other occasion.

Attach tags to cards using foam pads for a three-dimensional look if you don't want them to swing.

- Cream card blank 69 x 184mm (2¾ x 7¼in)
- Decorative paper or card
- Card in coordinating plain colours ■ Eyelets and eyelet setter tools
- Circle cutter or 2.5cm (1in) circular punch ■ Stickers or other embellishments
- Coordinating ribbon

MULBERRY PAPER

Mulberry paper is wonderful. Delicate and almost transparent, it is very attractive, with long fibres running through it. It comes in a number of glorious colours and, being surprisingly strong, can be used in many exciting ways. When wet, mulberry paper tears easily to give the most fantastic feathery edges, making it a very decorative and versatile material for card making.

17 HEARTS AND FLOWERS

Tear mulberry paper to soften the edges and layer it for a delicate look. This delightful card has a simple geometrical design with love at its heart, ideal for get-well wishes. Tiny round gems add sparkle to the flowers and lift the spirits.

■ 100 x 100mm (4 x 4in) white card blank ■ Mauve card
■ Mulberry paper in white, pink and three shades of mauve
■ Scraps of white paper or card ■ Heart and flower
punches ■ Round silver mini gems

1 Cut a 10 x 10cm (4 x 4in) square of mauve card and stick it to the front of the white card blank (or use a mauve card blank).

2 Use a fine watercolour brush and water to 'paint' an 8cm (3in) square on white mulberry paper, using a ruler as a guide. Position the ruler up to the wet lines and tear the paper along them to produce a square with a feathered edge.

3 Tear three 2cm (¾in) squares from each of your mauve mulberry papers in the same way.

Use glue stick or another type of 'dry' glue to attach the mulberry paper pieces to the card because wet glue weakens it and the wet paper could easily tear.

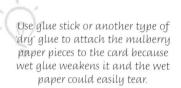

4 Punch out eight white paper or card flowers and stick a tiny round gem in the centre of each one.

5 Punch out one pink paper heart, sandwiching the mulberry paper between thin paper for a sharper punch.

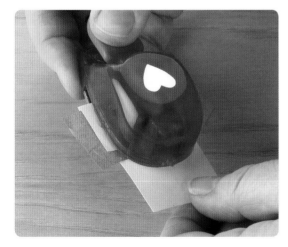

6 Stick the white mulberry paper to the centre of the card front. Stick the small mauve squares in a grid pattern on the top then stick on the paper flowers and finally add the heart to the centre square.

18 FLOWERS OF THE FIELD

Tear mulberry paper freely to capture the natural look of flower petals. Roughly torn mulberry paper flowers in glorious red echo the delicacy of wild poppies in a golden cornfield.

1 Draw the shapes of the flowers and leaves faintly in pencil on mulberry paper – use red for the petals, black for the flower centres and green for the leaves and sepals. Paint over the lines with water then tear them out carefully.

2 Cut stalks out of green mulberry paper and stick them in position on the gold-coloured paper. Add the flowers, leaves and sepals, using the photograph here as a guide or making your own arrangement.

3 Stick the decorated gold paper centrally on the front of the card blank to finish.

■ Red card blank 104 x 152mm (4 x 6in) ■ Mulberry paper – red, black and green ■ Gold coloured paper 14 x 9cm (5½ x 3½in)

When tearing fine shapes from mulberry paper, ease the paper apart sideways where possible, rather than pulling forward and back – this creates softer edges.

■ 14.5 x 21cm (5¾ x 8¼in) rectangle of gold card ■ Paper in black and white ■ Mulberry paper – red, yellow and green ■ Small star punch

19 STAR OF WONDER

Layer mulberry paper over white card for a stained-glass effect. The translucency of mulberry paper means that when placed over a white background the colours seem to glow.

1 Score and fold the rectangle of gold card to make a 14.5 x 10.5cm (5¾ x 4in) card blank. Cut a square of black paper 8.5cm (3¼in) and use the template on page 106, to remove the shapes using a craft knife.

2 Cut mulberry paper shapes slightly larger than the template shapes and stick them to the back of the black paper to create your window design. Stick white paper over the back of the design and then glue the whole thing to the front of your gold card.

3 Cut a narrow strip of black paper to the width of the card. Using the star punch, cut four evenly spaced stars from the black paper strip. Back the strip with yellow mulberry paper and then white paper then stick the strip across the bottom of the card to finish.

Use white pencil to draw your design on black paper to show up clearly.

20 IN THE FRAME

Cover slide frames with mulberry paper to create pretty picture windows for a delightful birthday card. Flexible as well as attractive, mulberry paper makes a perfect covering. Use rubber stamps to decorate it and to create pictures in the centre of the frames, then add flower-shaped gems for extra sparkle.

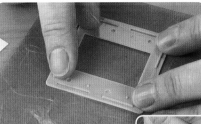

1 Stick a slide mount face down on to a piece of pink mulberry paper, as shown.

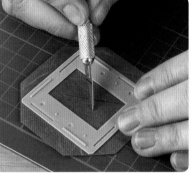

2 Cut around it, leaving a 1.5cm (½in) border and trim the corners diagonally. Make a cut diagonally inside the aperture, as shown.

3 Wrap the paper around the sides of the frame and stick down – you may need to trim the central points to reduce bulk.

4 Repeat steps 1–3 to cover two more slide frames, then, using a gold inkpad and leaf stamp, stamp motifs over the frames.

5 Cut three 4.5cm (1¾in) squares of white mulberry paper and stamp a single gold motif in the centre of each one. Stick each one to a 4.5cm (1¾in) square of white card. Stick a small flower gem to each stem for embellishment.

6 Stick one of your flower pictures behind each frame then stick the three frames on to a piece of textured card, using foam pads to raise them off the surface. Trim the card evenly all round so it will fit on the card blank and stick down.

When sticking mulberry paper down, always apply glue to the whole surface to prevent loose spots and maintain an even transparency.

■ Card blank 100 x 210mm (4 x 8¼in) ■ 3 slide mounts
■ Mulberry paper in pink and white ■ White card
■ Textured card ■ Gold ink pad ■ Small leaf stamp
■ 3 flower gems

BEADS

Beads are so beautiful that I love using them on my cards. From the tiniest accent beads to large beads that can be used as focal points, they add extra dimension and texture to cards and can be so very decorative and stylish. There are beads for just about every occasion, and they can be used in many different ways.

21 CAREER LADDER

For texture and colour in an instant, sprinkle beads on to double-sided tape. The beads stick to the tape like glue. Here gold beads were stuck to a tape ladder, which was then trimmed with suitable motifs. This easily adaptable idea was used here for a new job card.

- Brown card blank 100 x 210mm (4 x 8¼in)
- Double-sided tape 0.5cm (¼in) wide ■ Gold accent beads ■ Scraps of paper and card, small beads and wire for the decorations

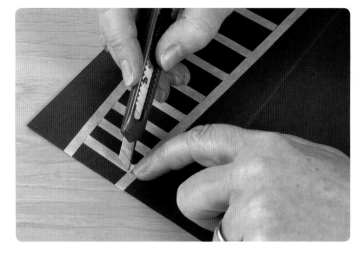

1 Mark out a ladder in pencil on the front of the card, 5cm (2in) wide at the top and 7.5cm (3in) wide at the bottom. Make the rungs closer together at the top than at the bottom. Use a ruler to ensure that your lines are straight. Place a strip of double-sided tape along each line. Don't overlap the tape – use a craft knife to trim any overlapping edges, as shown left.

Small beads can roll a long way, so it is wise to work over a tray or piece of soft cloth to keep stray beads under control.

2 Peel off the backing from the tape and tip the gold beads all over it. When all the tape is covered collect the surplus beads and return them to the container. Use a paintbrush to wipe up any loose beads around the edges of the lines.

3 Cut along the right-hand edge of the ladder, leaving a narrow border of card – use a ruler and craft knife for this, with a cutting mat underneath.

Cut or punch a green bottle shape from card and add gold paper around the neck and as a label. Thread gold beads on to wire, and attach the wire to the back of the bottle.

Stick bead 'bubbles' down the side of the card.

Cut an aperture in folded orange card and place white paper inside. Add a few scribbles to suggest writing.

4 Stick the embellishments in place on the ladder as shown above and right. Allow these to overlap the edge of the ladder but make sure they do not protrude beyond the edge of the card back.

Make a blue paper folder and wrap red wool or thread around the corners.

Use particularly attractive beads as your focal points. Here three lovely heart beads send a message of love for a wedding or engagement.

Add three-dimensional detailing with selective beading. This adorable brown mouse looks especially cute with his beady eyes and nose and would make a lovely birthday card for a child.

- Pink card blank 69 x 184mm (2¾ x 7¼in)
- Cream pearlescent card and pink card ■ Pink and cream rose-patterned paper ■ Three heart-shaped flat-backed glass beads, 2cm (¾in) long

Look out for unusual beads on old necklaces in junk shops and charity stores.

1 Cut a 14 x 3.5cm (5½ x 1½in) panel of cream card. Cut a pink rectangle fractionally larger and stick the cream card centrally on top.

2 Stick the three hearts down the centre of the cream panel using Glue Dots or small pieces of double-sided tape.

3 Cut a panel of patterned paper slightly smaller than the card blank front and stick it in place then stick the decorative panel in the centre to finish.

- Dark green card blank 100 x 100mm (4 x 4in) ■ Green daisy-pattern paper and yellow decorative paper ■ Light brown felt or velvet paper ■ Flower punch ■ Seed beads in green, red, black and pink ■ Pink ribbon ■ Fine beading needle that will pass through the beads ■ White thread

It can be tricky to stitch through card. Make it easy for yourself by piercing guide holes with a sturdy needle before you begin.

1 Cut a 7.5cm (3in) square of green patterned paper and stick it centrally on the dark green card. Cut the mouse shapes from felt and paper (see the template on page 106). Punch a flower shape from yellow paper.

2 Arrange the pieces to make the mouse, adding ribbon for a tail and gluing on beads for the buttons, nose and eyes. Add the whiskers by making long stitches with white thread.

3 Thread up some green beads for the flower stalk and stitch to the card. Stick on the flower and then stitch red beads in the centre.

24 PARCEL POST

For a striking bithday card, add strings of beads to areas of your design for rapid detailing. You don't have to stitch beads on individually – for quick results string a few on to your thread and attach them in one go.

- White card blank 69 x 184mm (2¾ x 7¼in) ■ Duo paper (plain on one side, patterned on the other) ■ Seed beads ■ Silver thread ■ Fine beading needle and sturdy needle for making holes in the card

1 Cut a piece of patterned paper fit the front of the card. On the reverse, mark with pencil every 6cm (2¼in) along one long side. Mark the opposite side at 3cm (1⅛in), 6cm (2¼in) further along and then another 6cm (2¼in) further along. Draw pencil lines between the marks to create zigzags, then cut along the lines to make triangles.

2 Trim 0.5cm (¼in) from the shortest side of three triangles and turn these over to use the plain side.

3 Cut five 2cm (¾in) squares from spare patterned paper to make the parcels. Stick each square in a triangle – a plain square on two patterned triangles and a patterned square on three plain triangles.

4 Use a sturdy needle to make holes in and around each parcel – one in the centre, one halfway along each edge, and one slightly above and to each side of the top centre hole for the bow.

5 Fix the end of a length of fine silver thread at the back of one triangle with sticky tape and push the needle through at one side of the square. Thread on four beads and push the needle down the centre hole. Continue to stitch on beads in this way to make the parcel ties, finishing at the top.

6 Add two lengths of thread with two beads at each side of the top to create the bow loops then thread on three beads; take the thread over the end bead and back through the other two beads to hang down from the bow. Repeat on the other side of the bow.

7 Stick the triangles and the top and bottom pieces on to the card – there will be a white space between the triangles. Finally, stitch beads at 2cm (¾in) intervals along the card fold for added decoration.

When stitching beads along a fold, take the opportunity to stitch in an insert at the same time for that extra touch of class.

PAINTS, CRAYONS AND PENCILS

Most art shops are packed with a mouth-watering array of colours in the form of paints, inks, pens, pencils or crayons that can be used in all sorts of exciting ways to transform your cards. Use them to colour your work, highlight embellishments or create focal images on paper, card or fabric. The possibilities are endless.

25 SUPER SKATER

Discover how to use gutta and silk paints to create a shimmering design. Painting on silk is easier than you might think. Simply trace a design on to the fabric using gutta then colour in the shapes with silk paint. Drop salt on to damp areas to create wonderful patterns and add punched paper shapes as a finishing touch. This skating penguin makes a great Christmas motif.

- White three-fold aperture card blank 144 x 144mm (5¾ x 5¾in) with a 100mm (4in) square aperture
- Piece of mount-board or firm cardboard 15cm (6in) square to use as a painting frame ■ Shimmer paper
- 13cm (5in) square of white silk ■ Silver-coloured gutta
- Arctic blue, lemon and black silk paints ■ Silk painting salt ■ Narrow double-sided tape
- Snowflake punch

1 Using a craft knife, cut an 11cm (4½in) square aperture in the centre of the mount-board.

2 Use masking tape to fix the silk firmly and tautly across the aperture.

Hold designs up to the light after drawing gutta outlines to check that there are no breaks in the lines that would let paint through. This works especially well with clear gutta, which is otherwise difficult to see.

3 Tracing from the template on page 106, lightly draw the design on the silk in pencil.

4 Draw over the outline of the design using silver gutta, with the tip of the tube barely touching the silk. Move your hand steadily and smoothly, and squeeze the tube very gently. Don't leave any gaps in the lines, however minute. Allow the gutta outline to dry completely.

5 Use a brush to touch black silk paint within the silver lines of the penguin – the paint will spread outwards to meet the lines of gutta. Add tiny touches of yellow paint, as shown, remembering that it will spread.

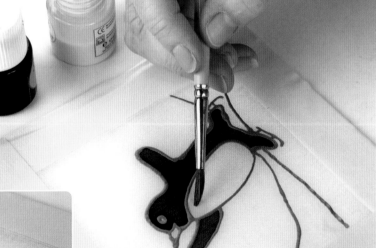

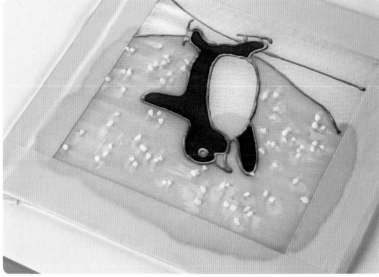

6 Paint the blue background, working quickly and not allowing the edges of the paint to dry before you finish. While the paint is still damp, scatter salt over it and leave it to dry. Tip off the salt, remove the silk from the mount-board and iron the silk to fix the colour.

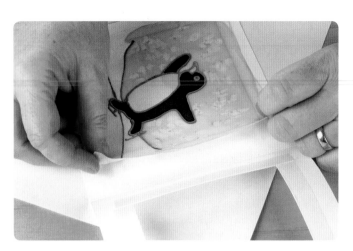

7 Stick the silk to the inside of one card flap using double-side tape so that when the card is folded the picture is behind the aperture. Stick the flap with the aperture to the backing flap to enclose the silk neatly.

8 Punch out 8–10 snowflakes from the shimmer paper and stick these around the edge of the aperture, overlapping the edges of the card and the silk painting randomly.

9 Trim any bits of snowflake that go beyond the edge of the card using a craft knife to finish.

26 MISTS OF TIME

Use the flowing, blending qualities of watercolour to create a magical scene for the man in your life. Use watercolour to create an abstract image, as here, or to paint a scene.

Use a hair dryer to dry watercolour paint quickly. If you aim at very wet paint you can even blow it over the paper to produce some exciting effects.

■ Rectangle of dark green card 20 x 21cm (8 x 8¼in) ■ Watercolour paper – any type and weight ■ Watercolour paints in a small selection of colours ■ Narrow dark green ribbon ■ Three small orange buttons

1 Mark a 16.5 x 2.5cm (6½ x 1in) block on watercolour paper in pencil. Within it paint irregular bands of light and dark shades of green and yellow, allowing the colours to spread. Leave to dry.

2 Score and fold the green card in half to make a 21 x 10cm (8¼ x 4in) card blank. Rub out the pencil marks on the watercolour paper and trim it to measure 19.5 x 7.5cm (7¾ x 3in) with the painting centred. Stick it centrally to the front of the green card.

3 Tie short lengths of narrow ribbon in the holes of three buttons and stick the buttons on the card to finish.

27 SOFT AND SIMPLE

Use a brass-rubbing technique to produce lovely soft motifs for your cards. This works especially well with handmade paper, as on this general greetings card.

- Rectangle of rusty brown card 20 x 21.5cm (8 x 8½in) ■ Thin white paper ■ White handmade paper ■ Small skeleton leaf
- Water-soluble crayons in yellow, mid and dark orange

1 Lay out a small skeleton leaf, rib side up, and cover with white paper. Gently rub over the leaf with a crayon, as shown.

2 Make three leaf rubbings altogether, each in a different colour, and cut them out neatly, following the outlines.

3 Using water and a brush, outline three rectangles, roughly 6.5 x 9cm (2½ x 3½in) on white handmade paper. Carefully tear out the rectangles. While the paper is still wet, draw orange and yellow crayons lightly along the edges then go over the colour with a damp paintbrush to blur the colour for a tinted effect. Leave to dry.

4 Stick a rubbed leaf motif in the centre of each rectangle. Score and fold the brown card to make a 10 x 21.5cm (4 x 8½in) card blank and then stick the three rubbed-leaf motifs along the front of the card to finish.

Practise the rubbing technique a few times on spare paper until you can achieve a fairly consistent effect.

28 FLOWER POWER

Use coloured pencils in warm colours to create unusual backgrounds and borders. Here the blocks, borders and patterns created with a few coloured pencils enliven a Mother's Day card.

Buy artist's quality coloured pencils for strong colours and excellent coverage.

- Cream card blank 104 x 152mm (4 x 6in) ■ Card in mid and dark orange ■ Decorative paper with sunflower motifs
- Artist's quality coloured pencils

1 Use artist's coloured pencils to draw wavy lines on a piece of mid orange card and from this cut a 10 x 2cm (4 x ¾in) strip and a 4cm (1½in) square. Stick the decorated card on to dark orange card and trim to leave a narrow border.

2 Cut out four paper sunflower motifs and tint with coloured pencils for added depth. Stick one sunflower in the square.

3 Scribble a close zigzag border around the edge of the card blank. Cut a 4 x 10cm (1½ x 4in) window in scrap card and use this as a stencil to scribble a yellow block on the lower right of the card.

4 Stick the wavy-line paper strip across the card over the scribbled block. Add the card square and sunflowers.

WIRE

Wire is a flexible and versatile material that can easily be formed into stunning shapes and now comes in some lovely colours. Add beads, sequins or charms to the wire for added style. As with so many crafts, there are a few basic tools you may need to buy, such as wire cutters or snips, but for many purposes you can improvise unless you wish to take your skills further.

29 ANIMAL MAGIC

Spring into action and coil wire to add bobbing three-dimensional decorations to this fun birthday card. The animal faces on this card are easily created, mainly with circles made from scraps of paper or card. If you prefer, you can use stickers, punched shapes or die-cuts instead.

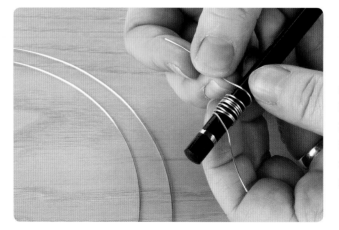

■ Purple card blank 100 x 210mm (4 x 8¼in) ■ Grey, pink, orange, white and brown card ■ Yellow card ■ Patterned yellow wrapping paper and plain yellow paper ■ Yellow ribbon ■ Black and white gel pens ■ Silver 24-gauge wire ■ Wire cutters or snips ■ Round-nosed pliers, if possible ■ Star punch

Use other tube-shaped items to make springs in other diameters – knitting needles are ideal for springs of all sizes.

1 Cut three 30cm (12in) lengths of silver wire using wire cutters or snips. Leaving a straight section 2–3cm (1in) long at the beginning, start to wind the first piece of wire around a pencil, as shown.

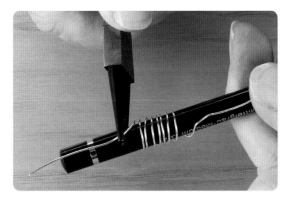

2 Complete the spiral, leaving another 2–3cm (1in) straight section at the other end. Use the round-nosed pliers to bend the wire at right angles at each end, flat to the pencil. Make sure that the straight sections are in line, as shown above.

3 Using the templates on page 107 and the guidelines given right, cut out and assemble the animal faces, then add the features. The templates show how the basic shapes are layered together to make the animal faces.

4 Attach one straight end of wire to the back of each head using masking tape, ensuring that the spiral starts just at the bottom of the face.

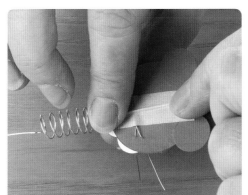

5 Make the parcel by covering a 7cm (3in) square of yellow card with patterned paper. Mitre the paper at the corners, as shown. Cut two 3 x 7cm (1¼ x 2¾in) box flaps from yellow paper. Fold one parallel with the long edge, right sides out, and stick it to the back of the parcel so the fold hangs over the top. Add a ribbon tie, using the photograph opposite as a guide.

To coordinate the card fully, use leftover paper from the box for the punched stars that decorate the background.

Layer the card pieces to create the animal faces, using the templates on page 107.

Make guide holes in the tiger's face for whiskers with a large needle, two on each side. Thread wire through the holes, arrange and trim to length.

Use a black gel pen for the features and a white gel pen to add highlights to the eyes, bringing the faces to life.

The monkey's face is made very simply by layering five circles to create the head, face, ears and mouth.

Stick the parcel to the card with foam pads to raise it up and add to the three-dimensional effect.

6 Attach the free end of each wire to the back of the parcel using tape, with the spring coming forward in front of the parcel. Decorate the card blank with stars punched from leftover paper. Position the box on the card and stick the second flap behind it. Stick the box on top.

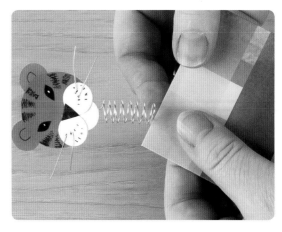

30 ABSOLUTELY CHARMING

String beads and charms on to wire to make splendid card toppers. The pretty embellishments on this wedding card look complicated but are really very simple to make.

■ White card blank 100 x 210mm (4 x 8¼in) ■ White textured card and pale turquoise card ■ Pearlescent paper ■ Wire in silver and gold ■ Crystal beads and turquoise glass beads ■ Four silver wedding charms ■ Narrow pale turquoise ribbon

1 Cut a piece of turquoise card to fit the front of the card blank. Cut a piece of white card slightly smaller, and a 6cm (2¼in) square of pearlescent paper. Frame the pearlescent paper with ribbon and stick it near the top of the white card.

2 Make a loop at the end of a length of silver wire. Put the wire through the hanging loop of one charm and twist the wire to hold it in place. Thread three turquoise beads on to the wire. Attach the other three charms at 5cm (2in) intervals, threading beads on the wire in between as before.

3 Wind the wire through the first loop to form a circle then wind the wire around the circle once more, adding crystal beads and fixing them and the other beads in place during the winding process.

4 Squeeze the wires at the positions of the charms to form corners, making the circle into a diamond shape. Fasten the wire shape across the paper square, stitching the wire to the card at the corners. (It helps if you make small holes in the paper at the stitch positions before you begin, as explained on page 54.)

5 Twist short lengths of gold wire together then form them into two rings. Tie with ribbon to hold them together then fix them in place on the paper square.

6 Add two lengths of ribbon lower down the white card, folding the ends to the back. Stick the white card to the pale turquoise card then stick that to the front of the card blank to finish.

When attaching charms on to wire, twist the wires loosely so that the charms can dangle down.

Vary the colour of the beads, ribbon and pearlescent paper to match the colour theme for the wedding. This card would look great in pink, lilac, or even gold.

31 STAR PLAYER

Wind wire around card to make a shimmering star to celebrate a sporting achievement. A gold wire star placed on a super paper rosette and set the rosette wobbling on a wire coil.

- Green card blank 144 x 144mm (5¾ x 5¾in) ■ Blue paper and white paper ■ Scraps of white card and green card ■ Gold 28-gauge wire ■ Circle cutter

1 Cut three blue circles 8.5cm, 8cm and 3.5cm (3¼in, 3in and 1¼in) in diameter. Cut notches around the largest circle and stick it over the mid-sized circle. Cut two white circles 6cm and 5.5cm (2½in and 2¼in) in diameter and repeat the notching and sticking process.

2 Stick the white circles centrally on the blue ones and add the smallest blue circle in the centre. Cut two tails from blue paper, 10cm and 11cm (4in and 4¼in) long and smaller ones from white paper; notch the ends and stick them behind the rosette.

3 Cut a 2.5cm (1in) circle of white card, cut six evenly spaced notches around it and wind it with gold wire. Wind the ends together at the back and stick the card to the centre of the rosette.

4 Trim off the top-right corner of the card front diagonally. Cut a length of wire and wind it twice around a glue stick to create a shallow spring. Use this to attach the rosette to the card as in card 29.

5 Make holes for the cross stitch with a needle, push wire through and fasten it at the back. Cover the backs of the wires with green card.

Use short lengths of wire for the stitching – they are less likely to get kinks and knots and can be joined by twisting at the back.

32 PROUD PEACOCK

Wind colourful wires into curls and swirls making lovely three-dimensional decorations for this all-purpose card. Here beads and wire represent the tail feathers of a peacock.

Use double-sided tape to hold the first few wires in position for the tail, then add layers of glue as you build up layers of wire.

- White card blank 104 x 152mm (4 x 6in) ■ Silver 24-gauge wire ■ Turquoise, blue and mauve 28-gauge wire ■ Turquoise beads, plus a few in blue, pink or iridescent colours ■ Turquoise inkpad ■ Diamond Glaze or similar dimensional adhesive ■ Blue or turquoise card ■ Circle cutter ■ Blunt-nosed pliers ■ Wire cutters or snips

1 Thread turquoise beads on to a 30cm (12in) length of silver wire, leaving about 5cm (2in) with no beads at one end (curl over the other end tightly to prevent the beads falling off).

2 Wind 20cm (8in) of the wired beads tightly into a circle and stick this to a 3cm (1¼in) circle of blue or turquoise card with Diamond Glaze. Leave to dry.

3 Cut 5–10cm (2–4in) lengths of coloured wire and curl the ends with pliers or string on beads. Stick the wires to the card to form the tail feathers. Ink the edges of the card with the inkpad.

4 Stick the beaded circle to the card and curve the remaining beads on the wire to form the peacock's neck and head, bending the end of the wire back on itself to form a beak. Use turquoise wire to form the bird's head feathers.

RIBBON

Ribbon can be used to embellish cards in a host of exciting ways. It comes in so many different thicknesses, finishes, colours and designs and can be put to practical as well as decorative uses. Collect attractive ribbons whenever you see them because they have so many applications. Look out for ready-made ribbon embellishments, too, which can add the finishing touch to a card.

33 HOME PATCH

Use adhesive ribbons to decorate your cards in an instant. Here they have been applied to random paper shapes to create a brilliant crazy-patchwork design to wish luck in a new home. Add buttons and charms of your choice to suggest personal wishes or interests or simply to echo the home theme.

■ White card blank
144 x 144mm (5¾ x 5¾in)
■ White paper ■ Scraps
of coloured and decorative
papers ■ Adhesive ribbons
■ Charms and buttons

1 Draw a 15 x 15cm (6 x 6in) square on white paper. Divide it up into a variety of triangles and number each one.

2 Trace or photocopy the design and mark the numbers on each shape. Cut out the shapes carefully.

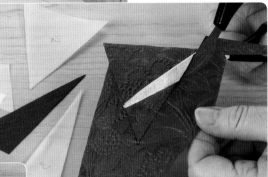

3 Use the paper triangles as templates to cut out triangles from fancy papers. Number each piece with its template number on the back to prevent confusion.

4 Stick the triangles on to the corresponding numbered triangle on the white paper. Trim the edges of the paper to exactly the size of the card.

5 Cover the joins between the triangles with adhesive ribbon, trimming the ends so that they meet neatly and making sure there aren't bulky overlaps.

Cut adhesive ribbon to length then peel the backing from one end and stick in place. Gradually remove the backing and press the ribbon in place. This helps prevent the ribbon sticking to itself.

6 Glue buttons and charms to the centres or corners of some triangles, using strong glue. Stick the whole thing to the front of the card blank.

34 WOVEN CROSS

Weave coordinating ribbons together and then place them behind an aperture for a truly elegant Easter card. Cut the aperture in a simple shape or use a punch to do it for you.

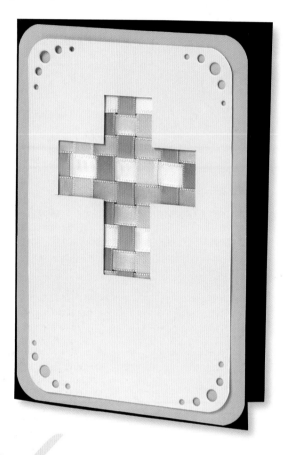

■ Green card blank 104 x 152mm (4 x 6in) ■ White card ■ Green, grey and white satin ribbon 7mm (¼in) wide ■ Rounded corner punch and eyelet hole punch or decorative corner punch of your choice

1 Cut a cross in a 13 x 8cm (5¼ x 3¼in) rectangle of white card, positioning it above centre. Draw a box around the cross in pencil then stick double-sided tape around the edge of the box.

2 Cut ribbons to the length and width of the box and weave them together, using the double-sided tape to stick them down.

3 Turn the white card over, round off the corners and punch holes at each corner following the curve – or simply use your chosen corner punch. Stick the card to the green card blank.

When weaving with ribbons to go behind apertures, position the first ribbon in the centre then position the ribbons on each side. That way your weaving will be perfectly centred in the aperture too.

35 LOVELY IN LAVENDER

Use ready-made ribbon flowers on an embossed card for super-quick results. Pep up the flowers with little tails of beads and ribbons and simply glue them in the frames on the card.

■ Pearlescent card blank 69 x 184mm (2¾ x 7¼in) with four squares down the front ■ Two white and two lilac satin ribbon roses ■ White pearl seed beads ■ 30cm (12in) of white ribbon 3mm (⅛in) wide ■ 30cm (12in) of purple ribbon 3mm (⅛in) wide

Can't find ribbon roses in the colour you want? Make your own by folding ribbon in half lengthways and then coiling it. Stitch to secure then add two ribbon loops in green for the leaves.

1 Cut a length of white ribbon approximately 15cm (6in) long. Tie a knot at one end and thread 10 beads on to it. Tie a knot at the other end and move five beads to each end.

2 Make several small loops with the ribbon in the centre and stitch the ribbon to a lilac rose so that the beads and loops hang down just below the flower.

3 Make and attach beaded tails to the remaining three roses then stick a rose in each square frame, alternating the colours.

36 JINGLE BELLS

Arrange ribbons behind an aperture to capture the lovely look of Iris folding. Bell shapes were chosen here for the apertures for a Christmas theme. Decorative ribbon bows applied on top of the apertures provide added embellishment and add an extra dimension.

1 Using the bell template from page 110, cut three bell-shaped apertures evenly spaced down the front of the card blank. Work carefully, using a craft knife on a cutting mat. Trace the folding template from page 110 on to paper.

2 Place the first aperture centrally over the folding template. If necessary, use a little low-tack tape to hold it in place. Position a short length of red ribbon over line 1 along one edge and stick it in place. Repeat along the other edges, overlapping pieces as necessary and trimming off the excess ribbon.

3 Lay a piece of orange ribbon over line 2 of the template on one edge and stick in place. Continue working round the template as before.

If you can't get satin ribbons in specific colours, you may be able to get paper ribbons from a florist or cut your own from strips of paper. (Thin paper should be folded in half and the fold placed on the visible edge in the aperture.)

4 Apply the gold ribbon in the same way, then the lemon ribbon, as shown. Stick a small piece of gold paper over the remaining gap at the centre. Repeat to fill the remaining apertures.

- Green card blank 69 x 184mm (2¾ x 7¼in)
- Red, orange, gold and lemon satin ribbons 7mm (¼in) wide ■ Festive red ribbon 7mm (¼in) wide or three ready-made ribbon bows ■ Gold paper ■ White card insert to fit the card blank

5 Fit an insert into the card, sticking it to the back of the card front to cover the backs of the ribbons.

6 Stick bows at the top of each bell made from red festive ribbon to finish.

Photographs

Use photographs to give your cards a personal and professional touch. Whether it is a family photograph for Christmas or photos of your garden flowers for like-minded friends, using your own photographs makes a card unique. Don't discard photos that are less than perfect – if they have successful elements you can cut out and use these (see card 38).

37 Going for Gold

Put the recipients in the picture, framing up 'then' and 'now' photos. This is a popular idea for birthdays these days, but here it has been used mark a 50th wedding anniversary. All the decorations are painted gold, so you can start with any assortment as long as the shapes work well. Add romantic embossed hearts with a touch of gold for the perfect finish.

1 Emboss a pattern in the top right-hand and bottom left-hand corners of the card. Here the design is one of hearts.

- Dark cream card blank 104 x 152mm (4 x 6in)
- Embossing stencil of your choice
- Embossing tool ■ Two slide frames ■ Selection of buttons and beads in any colours to decorate the frames ■ Gold acrylic paint

2 'Gild' the embossing by picking out some of it with a little gold paint using a small to medium sized paintbrush.

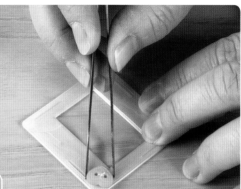

3 Stick a selection of beads, buttons, charms and any other embellishments on each slide frame to make an attractive and romantic decoration. Tweezers are helpful here for placing the small items.

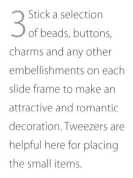

Never cut up your original photographs. Get them copied and use these for your cards instead.

4 Paint the slide frames with gold paint, covering all the decorations. Use two thin coats of paint rather than one thick one, leaving the paint to dry after each application.

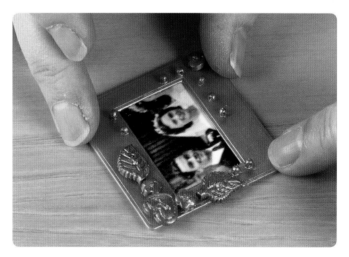

5 Cut out and stick your chosen photographs behind the frames. Ideally choose close-up images so you can include the greatest amount of detail.

6 Stick the frames in position on the card. In this case the 'before' photo was placed in the top left and the 'after' photo in the bottom right with the embossed motifs filling in the gaps.

38 MOSAIC MASTERPIECE

Cut photos of plants or flowers into squares to make a dramatic mosaic card. Use seasonal plants to celebrate summer, Easter, harvest or Christmas.

■ Cream card blank 144 x 144mm (5¾ x 5¾in) ■ Four photographs of flowers or plants with coordinating colours or themes

Pick photographs for mosaics based on their pattern and colour, without worrying about specific images.

1 Cut your photographs into 2.5cm (1in) squares; you need at least 25. Try to get a mix of squares with complete flowers or sprays, and squares that have more abstract patterns of flowers or foliage. A trimmer or guillotine makes cutting easy.

2 Lightly mark a 14cm (5½in) square on the front of the card with pencil to help you position the squares.

3 Play around with your squares until you have an interesting arrangement of 5 x 5 squares. Large flowers can be spread over several squares, like the peony on the featured card. The squares should fit within your frame with just a narrow space between them. Stick the squares in position then rub off the pencil marks.

39 CHRISTMAS GREETINGS

Use a good family portrait as the basis of your card. Shapes cut from a double-sided adhesive sheet and covered with glitter create a festive frame on this Christmas card.

■ A4 (US letter) sheet of dark green card ■ Double-sided adhesive sheet ■ Fine glitter in red, green and gold

1 Cut an 18 x 25cm (7 x 10in) rectangle from green card and score and fold it to create an 18 x 12.5cm (7 x 5in) card blank with the fold at the top.

2 Draw festive shapes on the back of the adhesive sheet, cut them out and stick the shapes in the top-left and bottom-right corners of the card. Peel the backing paper from the shapes and tip glitter on to them, one colour at a time, masking the other parts of the shape as you do so, then shake off the surplus.

3 Cut very narrow strips of adhesive sheet and use these to make borders between the shapes and the two free corners. Add glitter to these as before.

4 Lay your photo centrally on the card and lightly mark with a pencil around the edges. Using a craft knife and cutting mat cut around the edges of the shapes where they face the centre of the card, up to the point where they cross the pencil lines. Do not cut along the pencil lines. Rub out the pencil marks. Carefully position the photograph on the card, slipping two corners into the cuts you have made in the card.

Get lots of prints of your favourite photo and make several cards at the same time for family and friends.

40 GARDEN HARVEST

Take a leaf out of scrapbook styling and build a card design around photographs on a theme.
Use your own photos or supplement them with sticker photos, available from scrapbook suppliers. This is an ideal birthday card for a keen gardener.

- White card blank 144 x 144mm (5¾ x 5¾in)
- Dark green card and white card ■ Two coordinating patterned papers ■ Four garden-themed photographs (see step 2 for sizing) ■ Three dragonfly brads
- 30cm (12in) of beige rickrack braid ■ Three buttons in shades of green ■ Raffia

If you are short of a photograph, use some text or a suitable rubber-stamped image instead. If necessary you can also cut one photo into two.

1 Cut a piece of green card to fit the front of the card blank. Cut a 9cm (3½in) square from each patterned paper and stick the squares in the top-left and bottom-right corners of the green card, about 0.5cm (¼in) from the edges.

2 Mat the photographs with white and green card, making one photograph 7 x 5.5cm (2¾ x 2¼in) and the other three 3.5cm (1½in) square.

3 Cut two narrow strips of patterned paper and stick one 1cm (³⁄₈in) from the right edge and one the same distance from the bottom edge. Stick rows of rickrack braid on the card.

4 Position the small photographs down the right-hand side and the larger one in the top left, covering the ends of the braid, as shown in the photograph of the finished card.

5 Position the three dragonfly brads and fix them to the front of the card.

6 Tie raffia into the buttons and stick the buttons in place, one at each end of the bottom paper strip, and one just below the main photograph.

7 Add any other decorations as desired to suit your chosen theme.

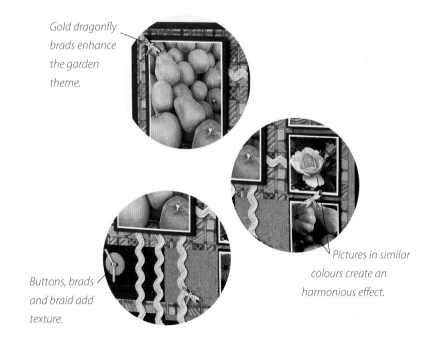

Gold dragonfly brads enhance the garden theme.

Buttons, brads and braid add texture.

Pictures in similar colours create an harmonious effect.

RUB-ONS

The best thing about rub-ons is that they give you wonderful detail with very little effort. They are easy to transfer to your cards, have a fantastic finish and are pretty much all you need to make a great card. They are also very versatile and can be used as they are or cut up and combined with other rub-ons. Choose them as the main focus of a card or for borders – there are endless possibilities.

41 MAGIC CIRCLES

Build a card design around a set of rub-ons – it's easy and fun to do. Rub-ons usually come on sheets containing coordinating designs. Pick a sheet and you are ready to go.

- Light, mid and dark mauve card ■ Rub-on flowers
- ■ Circle cutter

When applying a rub-on transfer, pay extra attention to the top edge, and pull the paper gently away from this first. If it is well stuck down it makes it easier for the rest. If any of the transfer comes away simply lower it back on to the card and rub over it again.

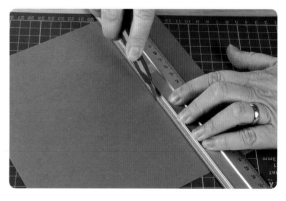

1 Cut a 15 x 30cm (6 x 12in) rectangle from dark mauve card, measuring and cutting carefully with a knife and ruler on a cutting mat. Score and fold the card in half to make a 15cm (6in) square card blank.

2 From mid mauve card cut three circles measuring 6cm, 7.5cm and 11cm (2¼in, 3in and 4¼in) in diameter. From light mauve card cut three circles 4.5cm, 6cm and 9.5cm (1¾in, 2½in and 3¾in) in diameter.

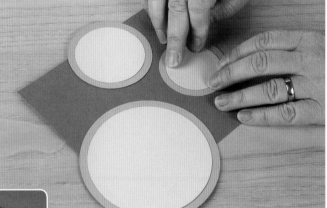

3 Stick each light mauve circle on to a slightly larger mid mauve circle. Stick the circles on to the front of the dark mauve card, allowing them to overlap the edges, as shown.

4 Using a ruler and cutting knife on a cutting mat, trim the edges of the circles in line with the card edges.

5 Cut out each rub-on flower and rub over it with the wooden stick or an embossing tool to transfer it to the centre of a circle. Make sure the largest flower goes on the largest circle, the smallest one on the smallest circle and so on.

6 Burnish each flower using the side of your thumb over the backing paper as shown left.

42 SAY IT WITH NUMBERS

Use rub-on numbers (or words) to get your message across. Here plenty of '18' rub-ons have been added to the background inside an aperture, along with a few appropriate motifs, for a fun 18th birthday card.

1 Rub '18's and suitable motifs randomly on to the bright green card front to form a background, noting roughly where the edges of the apertures will go so you don't waste any in areas that will be out of sight.

2 Cut a rectangle of dark green card to fit the card front. Cut a long rectangular aperture for the '1' about 1.5cm (⅝in) from the card fold. For the '8' cut two circles, one 7cm (2¾in) across at the bottom and a smaller one 5.5cm (2¼in), overlapping it at the top. Cut out smaller circles of the card 2cm (¾in) and 1.5cm (½in) across to position inside the number.

■ Bright green card blank 144 x 144mm (5¾ x 5¾in) ■ Dark green card ■ Rub-on numbers and motifs – as much of a variety as you can find

When using rub-ons to make backgrounds don't forget to vary the angles for variety – some could even be upside down.

3 Stick the dark green card over the light green card, and position the small circles in the larger circles, leaving the background to show through in the shapes of the 18.

43 PERFECT PARTY

Apply gold rub-ons to vellum to create stunning motifs. Apply smaller gold rub-ons to the card front directly for a change of pace and highlight your vellum motifs with additional trimmings.

- Pink card blank 104 x 152mm (4 x 6in) ■ Party rub-ons
- Spotted vellum ■ White baby rickrack braid
- Tiny pink paper flowers ■ 2.5cm (1in) square punch

1 Punch three 2.5cm (1in) square apertures evenly spaced down the right-hand side of the card front.

2 Cut spotted vellum slightly smaller than the card front and place it inside the card. Lightly mark the aperture positions on the vellum with pencil then remove it and transfer the rub-ons.

3 Erase your pencil marks and stick the vellum in place. Rub stars and streamers on to the front of the card and stick rickrack braid and flowers around the apertures to finish.

Open your card out before applying rub-ons to the front; this prevents the risk of making indents on the card back.

44 FAIRY RING

Use rub-ons to create three-dimensional borders. This one frames a delightful fairy that is also a rub-on. It has been transferred on to vellum to heighten its delicate look on this sweet birthday card.

- Pale green card blank or oval aperture card 104 x 152mm (4 x 6in)
- Dark green card ■ Pale green vellum ■ White paper
- Fairy rub-ons ■ Oval cutter

Use a pair of embroidery scissors for cutting around detailed shapes like the forms of the border rub-ons.

1 Cut an oval aperture in the front of your card unless it already has one. Rub the fruit and leaves on to dark green card and rub the small fairy on to green vellum.

2 Fix the green vellum behind the oval aperture and back it with white paper, cut to the size of the card.

3 Cut out the fruit and leaves and stick them around the aperture to form a border, using foam pads behind alternate shapes.

PUNCHES

Punching paper or card gives you repeatable, neat and accurate shapes that are decorative and versatile. The technique is great for creating lots of identical motifs that can be used as they are or layered for a three-dimensional effect. Punches can also make fancy holes in your cards. They come in all sorts of designs and sizes, are very easy to use, and can save a great deal of time and money.

45 SWIRLING LEAVES

Use small punched shapes to create both background pattern and colourful embellishments. Punched leaves in autumn colours tumble gently across this card to welcome the new season. Add golden details to the leaves to sparkle and shimmer against the misty background on this general-purpose card.

1 Stick wide masking tape to the non-stick paper and punch out leaf shapes. Peel off the masking tape shapes and stick them gently and randomly on the front of the card.

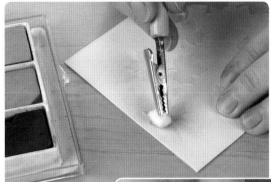

2 Dust over the shapes with orange chalk, pulling the chalk away from each leaf shape, as shown.

3 Peel off the leaf shapes carefully and stick them on in new positions. Punch new shapes from tape, if necessary.

4 Now dust over the leaf shapes with red chalk, again pulling the chalk away from the shapes. As before, remove the leaf masks gently.

5 Punch out leaves in a variety of autumnal colours. Use the gold gel pen to draw veins on the punched leaves.

To keep punches sharp, punch motifs from aluminium foil from time to time.

■ Cream card blank 104 x 152mm (4 x 6in) ■ Scraps of red, orange, yellow and brown paper or card ■ Orange and red chalks ■ Chalk applicator, sponge or cotton wool ■ Wide masking tape (good quality) ■ Scraps of non-stick paper (sticker backing paper is ideal) ■ Leaf punch ■ Gold gel pen

6 Stick the leaves in a swirling shape down the front of the card, overlapping some of them for a natural look.

46 FLOWER DIMENSIONS

Combine punched holes with punched motifs for a card with real impact. Here, punched flowers are covered with ornate Japanese paper and the same paper is used to back the holes for a super three-dimensional card for all occasions.

■ Pale green card blank 100 x 100mm (4 x 4in) ■ Patterned paper and white paper ■ Dark green card ■ Scrap of card ■ Eight sticky-backed gems ■ Small flower punch

1 Punch four flowers, equally spaced along the right-hand edge of the card front then stick patterned paper behind them. Stick some more patterned paper to scrap card and leave to dry. Punch four flower motifs from the covered card.

2 Cut simple stalk and leaf shapes from dark green card and stick them in position on the front of the card. Stick the four flower motifs at the tops of the stalks using foam pads and stick a gem to the centre of each flower shape.

3 Cut a white paper insert slightly smaller than the green card and stick it inside the card, covering the paper behind the holes.

Punch out a few extra shapes while you have your punches out, and keep them handy in a small container to create quick cards in the future.

47 TWO HEARTS AS ONE

Use border punches to give your cards romantic lacy edgings. Here a double border creates a lovely lacy effect that complements the gold hearts. Nothing goes to waste – the punched hearts from the border decorate the front of the card.

■ Paper in three shades of pink ■ Border punch ■ Two laser-cut gold hearts about 2.5cm (1in) high

Save even tiny punched shapes to use in shaker boxes (see page 62).

1 Cut a 20 x 15cm (8 x 6in) rectangle from dark pink paper and another from medium pink paper. Score and fold them in half to make a card 10 x 15cm (4 x 6in).

2 Punch a border along one 15cm (6in) edge of the medium pink rectangle and stick the paper over the dark pink rectangle. Save the punched-out hearts.

3 Cut an 11.5 x 15cm (4½ x 6in) rectangle of pale pink paper and punch along one long edge.

4 Score and fold along the other long edge of the paper 2.5cm (1in) from the edge. Stick this over the fold of the other papers so that the punched border is just above the punched border on the medium pink paper.

5 Stick laser-cut gold hearts on to the pale pink paper then stick the punched hearts made in step 2 around them, arranging them fairly randomly to look like confetti. Punch more medium-pink hearts and add these to the card too, completing the look.

48 ALL HANDS ON DECK

Use paddle punches to punch shapes from the centre of a card.
With a paddle punch you aren't limited to punching shapes close to the edges so make a punched design anywhere you like. Add punched shapes, sometimes overlapping, for a busy, lively look, and pick out one of the colours for a zingy border. This makes a great child's birthday card.

- Dark blue card blank 144 x 144mm (5¾ x 5¾in)
- Turquoise card ■ Bright paper in yellow, orange, red, dark blue and green ■ Hand and swirl paddle punch, hammer and mat

The edges of punched shapes are sometimes raised. Smooth them down with a bone folder.

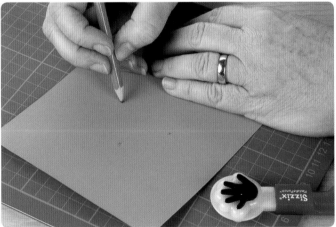

1 Cut a 12.5cm (5in) square of turquoise card and use a pencil to lightly mark the positions of four punched hand shapes at the centre, facing inwards. Marking the positions first will help to ensure a well-balanced effect.

2 Punch out the hand shapes using a paddle punch and hammer on a punching mat, as shown right. Make sure you have a hard surface underneath the mat to ensure a clean cut.

3 Punch out more hand shapes and some spirals from brightly coloured papers. Stick them on the turquoise square, overlapping them slightly in places.

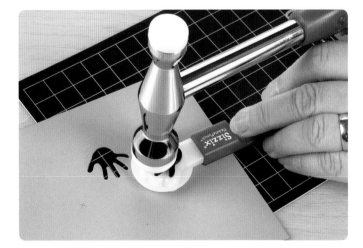

4 Stick the square centrally on to the front of the card blank. Cut narrow strips of yellow paper and stick them around the turquoise square to create a border, completing the card.

THREADS AND FIBRES

Traditionally used with fabrics, threads and fibres also work surprisingly well with paper and card. You can stitch the paper directly (see below and page 56) or use threads to attach tags, charms, ribbon motifs and other items, sticking the threads to the card for simplicity. You can even wrap the thread around card shapes (page 57), which is an art form all of its own, known as Spirelli.

49 SEW EASY

 Stitch a simple design on paper as the centrepiece of your card – there are no fraying edges to worry about. This versatile idea can easily be adapted. The flowers shown suit a lady, but what about an animal for a child's card, or chicks and eggs for Easter? The motifs in this book should provide plenty of ideas.

1 Cut a 6.5 x 10cm (2½ x 4in) rectangle of white card and a 7.5 x 11cm (2¾ x 4¼in) rectangle of green card. Trace the template from page 107 and place it over the white card so the design is centred. Use a pricking tool or pin to prick holes along the design lines for the stitches at the positions marked by dots.

■ White card blank 104 x 152mm (4 x 6in) ■ Pink and green checked paper ■ Card in green and in white ■ Stranded embroidery cotton (floss) in pink, blue and green ■ Embroidery needle ■ Two pearl seed beads ■ Pricking tool or pin and mat ■ Corner punch

2 Stitch the large flowers in lazy daisy stitch using two strands of pink thread. To do this, come up at the centre of the petal and go back down in the same hole, leaving a loop. Catch the loop with a small stitch at the opposite end, pulling the loop until it sits snugly on the paper. Stitch a pearl bead to the centre of each flower (see the tip below left).

Don't knot your threads on the back of the paper – this will create unsightly lumps. Instead secure the ends on the back with sticky tape.

3 Work the stems and leaves in three strands of green thread, using backstitch for the stems and lazy daisy stitch for the leaves.

4 Work the small flowers in two strands of blue thread – each flower comprises six straight stitches meeting at the centre.

5 Use the corner punch on every corner of the embroidered white card and then use it on the green card, as shown. Stick the embroidered white card centrally on the green card and leave it to dry completely.

6 Cut a piece of checked paper to fit the card front and stick it in place. Stick the stitched card centrally on top to finish.

50 HAUNTING HALLOWEEN

Embellish paper shapes with running stitch to create a wonderful patchwork effect. This card is made from orange and white shapes on a black background for Halloween.

1 Cut a 12.5cm (5in) square of orange card, and a 10cm (4in) square of black card. Trace the pumpkin and ghost templates from page 110 and use them to cut out two orange pumpkins and two white ghosts.

2 Pricking the holes first, stitch running stitches around each square and across the centre of the black square. Stitch around the shapes too then stick them in the four squares formed by the orange stitching on the black card square.

3 Stick the black square in the centre of the orange square then stick the whole lot on the front of the card blank.

■ Black card blank 144 x 144mm (5¾ x 5¾in)
■ Orange, white and black card ■ Black and orange thread ■ Pricking tool or pin and mat

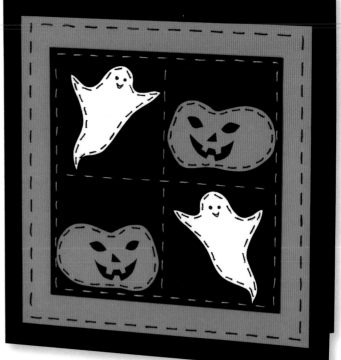

Mark light pencil lines on the back of the paper to guide you when you prick the stitching holes.

51 BABY FEET

Use soft fluffy fibres to frame a focal motif. Here a simple baby's footprint plaque forms the centrepiece.

1 Cut a 144 x 125mm (5¾ x 5in) piece of vellum and stick it to the card against the fold, applying glue to the corners and centre. Trim the card front to match the vellum.

2 Punch holes along the edge of the card and weave two lengths of fibre through each hole, tying a bow in the centre. Thread a button on to each thread end and stick it to the card with a Glue Dot. Thread a short length of thread through the remaining buttons and attach them too.

3 Cut a 7.5 x 9cm (3 x 3½in), rectangle of blue card with zigzag edging shears. Wind fibres around the corners of the card and tape to the back. Stick the plaque in the centre and stick the card to the vellum with sticky pads.

■ Pale blue card blank 144 x 144mm (5¾ x 5¾in) ■ Striped vellum ■ Small plaque ■ Turquoise mohair fibre ■ Pale blue buttons 1cm (½in) in diameter ■ Scrap of pale blue card ■ Zigzag edging shears ■ Eyelet punch

Fluffy fibres can be difficult to thread through holes. Wrap sticky tape around one end to help you.

52 SIMPLE SPIRELLI

Use Spirelli winding techniques to create pretty motifs for your cards. You can buy pre-cut forms for Spirelli work or cut your own shapes with a special punch, as here. Experiment with different winding orders to create a wide range of effects – it's lots of fun and very easy. This card would be great for a girl's birthday.

1 Punch out three Spirelli circles from the lilac card (or use ready-cut shapes). Punch three small flowers from the leather paper. Tape a length of variegated cotton (floss) to one large circle and pass it through a notch on the edge, as shown.

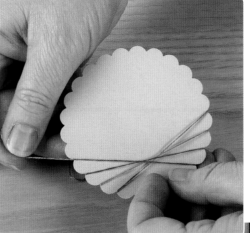

2 Count eight notches along and pass the thread through the notch to the back. Take the thread seven notches back and pass it to the front. Continue in this way to wind the thread around the shape to complete the circle. Tape the end securely on the back.

■ White card blank
100 x 210mm
(4 x 8¼in) ■ Lilac card
■ Purple leather paper
■ Variegated stranded
cotton (floss) in lilac blue
and pink
■ Small mauve gems
■ Circular Spirelli punch
7.5cm (3in) in diameter
and small five-petalled
flower punch

3 Wind a small punched flower with thread, securing it on the back with a tiny piece of tape. Stick it in the centre of the Spirelli circle. Repeat to decorate the remaining two circles.

4 Cut a rectangle of lilac card to fit the front of the white card blank and stick it in place. Cut a 19 x 8cm (7¾ x 3½in) piece of leather paper and stick it centrally on the lilac card.

5 Arrange the Spirelli circles on the card, using the photograph, left, as a guide. Stick them in place. Stick small mauve gems around the shapes to echo the outlines and fill in the gaps.

Sticker waste makes a good alternative to tape for fixing thread ends in place on the back of card shapes.

VELLUM

The lovely translucency of vellum can add something really special to a card. It's easy to use and comes in a growing range of designs, but crafters often have problems fixing it in place without the glue showing. There are ways to avoid this, as you will see, and the final results are well worth a little effort.

53 OCEAN WAVES

Use layers of vellum to create depth. This greetings card, perfect for a man who loves sailing, uses four colours of vellum – three for the boat and one for the sea. Where the waves overlap, they look darker, giving the sea greater depth.

Spread glue very thinly on vellum and leave it until it is almost dry before sticking the vellum down.

■ White card blank 104 x 152mm (4 x 6in) ■ Vellum in pale blue, rust, red and beige ■ Self-adhesive silver metal sheet ■ Self-adhesive silver border ■ Mid-blue chalk and applicator

1 Using a chalk applicator or cotton-wool ball, rub blue chalk on to the top quarter of the white card for the sky. Leave gaps for clouds.

2 Using the template on page 109, cut out the sails, hull and flag from coloured vellum and stick them in position, with the hull 10cm (4in) above the bottom edge of the card.

3 Cut an 11cm (4½in) square of pale blue vellum and cut a wavy edge along the top. Glue to the card around the sides and lower edge.

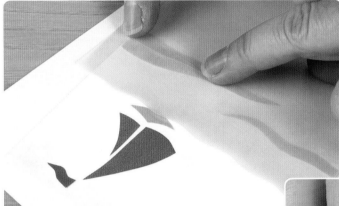

4 Cut wavy shapes from the blue vellum, and stick these here and there on the sea, coming in from the edges and overlapping in places. Apply glue to the waves at the edges of the card and at the ends.

5 Using the templates on page 109, cut the fish shapes from the silver sheet and stick them on to the blue vellum sea. Tuck some into the edges of the vellum waves. Use the fish to cover any visible glue marks.

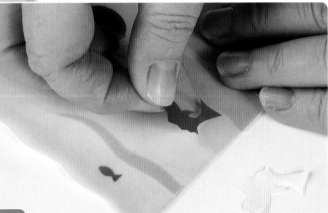

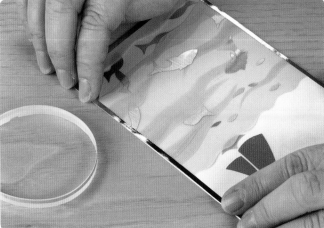

6 Trim off the excess vellum around the card then stick the self-adhesive border strips around the edges, covering the glue marks, to finish.

54 FLOWER FANCY

Use layers of punched vellum shapes to create three-dimensional embellishments. The vellum gives the shapes great delicacy and the liquid pearl centres on these flowers add sheen. This card would be especially wonderful as a wedding anniversary card.

1 Punch twelve flower shapes from pale pink vellum, and eight of your second flower shapes from white vellum. Using an embossing tool and resting on something soft, like craft foam, work gentle circles on the larger flower petals to shape them, as shown.

■ White card blank 100 x 100mm (4 x 4in) ■ Pale pink, pale green, shimmering white and patterned blue vellums ■ Liquid Pearls in pink ■ Silver gel pen ■ Two flower punches about the same size ■ Embossing tool or stylus ■ Soft surface, such as craft foam ■ Rounded corner punch ■ Sparkling clear heart-shaped gems

3 Place a blob of Liquid Pearls in the centre of each flower, as shown, and leave to dry.

2 Layer the flower shapes – three layers for the pink flowers and two for the white ones, and stick them together in the centre.

To punch out vellum shapes quickly, fold or cut the vellum into smaller pieces and then punch through several layers at once.

4 Draw and cut out 14 leaf shapes from green vellum. Draw silver veins on the leaves using the silver gel pen.

5 Cut out a square of blue patterned vellum slightly smaller than the card blank and round off the corners using the punch. Stick the vellum to the front of the card, using glue in the centre and at the corners.

6 Stick the leaves in a circle on the vellum then add the flowers. Finally, stick the gem hearts in the centre of the card, angling them slightly.

55 LOVE LETTER

Use vellum for envelopes – it gives an enticing hint of the contents. Here a textured heart is placed in a vellum envelope and mounted onto card, creating a striking Valentine's card.

■ Deep pink card blank 144 x 144mm (5¾ x 5¾in) ■ Pink corrugated card ■ Pale pink vellum and glittery patterned vellum ■ Pink glitter ■ Assorted sequins in silver, pink and purple

1 Using the templates on page 108, cut the envelope from pink vellum and the heart from pink corrugated card. Apply PVA glue to the edges of the envelope, sprinkle glitter over them and then shake off the surplus. Repeat on the heart. Allow them to dry.

2 Trim the top front of the card at an angle and add glitter as before. Cut a 7 x 15cm (2¾ x 6in) strip of glittery vellum and stick this to the card with a glittery edge at the top; trim off the excess.

3 Score, fold and stick the envelope where the edges meet. Place sequins and glitter inside.

4 Stick the heart in the envelope and attach the envelope to the card as shown in the photograph above.

Make a vellum envelope to contain your entire card using this same technique.

56 SHEER ABSTRACT

Apply overlapping vellum shapes for a geometrical design with depth. The vellum alters the colour of the card beneath and creates new shapes for a subtle effect, ideal for the man in your life.

Use a tiny spot of glue to attach the vellum where each eyelet will go to keep the vellum in place while you punch the eyelet hole.

■ White or blue card blank 100 x 210mm (4 x 8¼in) – see step 1 ■ Blue and rust-coloured papers ■ White, pale blue and pale turquoise vellums ■ Metallic eyelets ■ Eyelet setting tools

1 Cut blue paper to fit the front of the card blank and stick it in place (or use a blue card). Cut rust-coloured paper slightly smaller than the blue card.

2 From white vellum cut one rectangle 17 x 6cm (6¾ x 2¼in), another rectangle 6 x 9.5cm (2¼ x 3¾in) and a third rectangle 8.5 x 6cm (3¼ x 2¼in). From blue vellum cut four 2.5cm (1in) squares and two 1.2cm (½in) squares. From turquoise vellum cut two 2.5cm (1in) squares and two 1.2cm (½in) squares.

3 Attach the squares and rectangles to the rust-coloured paper rectangle in layers using the photograph as a guide and using eyelets to attach the large white vellum rectangles for added interest.

4 Stick the rust paper centrally on to the blue-covered card blank to finish.

CONFETTI

Use sequin confetti to add instant glamour and shine to your cards. You can use it as a small part of your design or make it the main focus of your card. It comes in shapes suitable for all occasions, some in fabulous colours, and a little goes a long way so it is great value.

57   HAVE A HEART

Make a confetti-filled shaker box to add a surprise element to your card. Here the shaker box contains silver heart confetti that seems to spill out and fall down the card front in a romantic cascade. This card will certainly convey your heartfelt message on Valentine's Day.

■ Cream card blank 100 x 210mm (4 x 8¼in)
Red card ■ Red patterned paper ■ Acetate ■ Silver heart-shaped confetti ■ Mini heart punch ■ Red slide mount in two halves

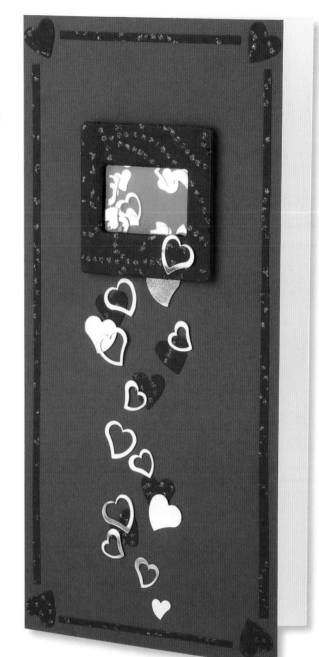

1 Cover one half of the slide frame with the red paper, referring to the instructions on page 25.

2 Cut a piece of acetate to fit the back of the frame and stick it in place. Stick the second half of the frame to the back of the acetate, covering the edges of the acetate completely.

3 Cut red card to fit the front of the card blank and place a small pile of confetti where the box will be on it. Stick the picture mount right side up on top, enclosing the confetti, as shown.

Make your own 'confetti' by saving small punched shapes made when creating punched borders, for example.

4 Punch heart shapes from the red patterned paper and stick five falling randomly below the box. Scatter silver confetti hearts over the red hearts and stick them down carefully where they fall.

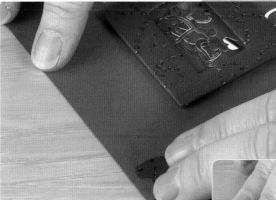

5 Stick a paper heart in each corner of the red card, as shown.

6 Cut very narrow strips of paper and use them to make a border around the card between the corner hearts.

7 Stick the decorated red paper rectangle on the card blank to finish.

58 BABY TED

Bond confetti with Angelina fibre to make a sparkling, translucent material that you can cut and shape. Here the new fabric is used for a teddy motif that repeats the shape of the confetti. The bear is cut from a template, but you can use a punched shape for speed, if desired. This is an ideal new baby card.

- Pale mauve card blank 104 x 152mm (4 x 6in)
- White vellum and heart-patterned vellum
- Baking parchment ■ Angelina fibre in mauve
- Teddy bear metallic confetti shapes ■ Fluffy mauve fibres ■ Embroidery needle ■ Heart punch (optional) ■ Mauve metallic gel pen

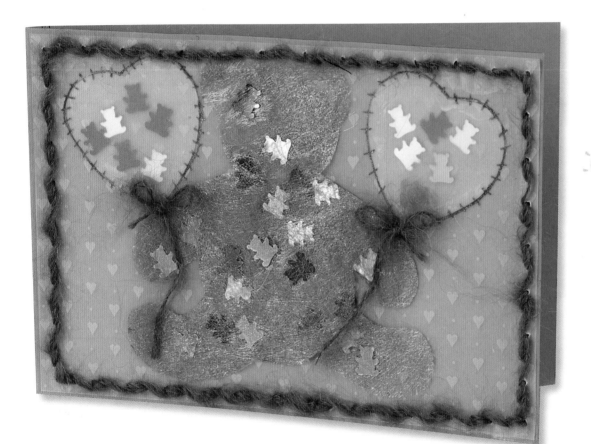

Before bonding confetti with Angelina fibres, place your template over it to check the positioning of the confetti.

1 Place a thin layer of Angelina fibres on a piece of baking parchment. Scatter teddy shapes on to the fibre then add another thin layer of fibres over them. Place a second piece of baking parchment on top.

2 Set an iron for silk and press the baking parchment for 2–3 seconds to bond the fibres together in a sheet. Allow it to cool.

3 Trace the teddy template on page 106 and use it to cut a teddy-bear shape from the sheet of fibre, trying to keep the small confetti teddies whole.

4 Cut a piece of patterned vellum and stitch it to the front of the card with mauve fibre, sticking it lightly first and pricking the holes before stitching. Stick the teddy shape in the centre.

5 Cut or punch two hearts from white vellum and arrange one on each side of the teddy as if they are balloons he is holding. Remove the hearts and stick a few teddy bear confetti shapes where the heart 'balloons' will go. Stick the hearts on top.

6 Draw around the heart shapes with the mauve gel pen and add 'stitches' across the lines.

7 Tie lengths of fluffy fibres into bows with a long tail and stick these in place on the hearts for the teddy to 'hold'.

59 TREE STAR

■ Turquoise card blank 144 x 144mm (5¾ x 5¾in) ■ Scraps of white mulberry paper ■ 40cm (16in) of dark green ribbon 1cm (½in) wide ■ 15cm (5in) length of white satin ribbon 1cm (½in) wide ■ Star confetti

Use confetti like tiny stickers to add ornament to your designs. So simple to make, all you need for this Christmas card is some ribbon for the tree and confetti for the ornaments.

1 Cut a 1cm (½in) piece of green ribbon. Cut the next piece 2cm (¾in) longer and the next one 2cm (¾in) longer still. Repeat until you have six pieces, the longest 11cm (4¼in). Cut a 2.5cm (1in) length for the trunk.

2 Stick the white ribbon along the bottom of the card, then stick the trunk and the other lengths on the card to form the tree. (Refer to the photograph as a guide.)

3 Stick star-shaped confetti along the branches of the tree, curving the lines to look like garlands and placing one star right at the very top. Stick scraps of white mulberry paper randomly around the tree for snow.

Rub confetti between your finger and thumb before sticking it down in case two pieces are stuck together.

60 TURKEY TROT

Use large pieces of confetti to create a sparkling centrepiece. With a seasonal border of golden leaves, this Thanksgiving card is quick and simple to make using confetti shapes.

1 Cut four 10 x 1.5cm (4 x ½in) strips of leafy paper and stick these around the edges of the card, a slight distance from the edge, to create a border.

2 Stick a confetti leaf in each corner where the paper borders cross.

3 Stick the six turkeys in two rows across the centre of the card.

Change the theme of your card simply by changing the confetti shapes – chicks on a green background would turn this into an Easter card.

■ Brown card blank 100 x 100cm (4 x 4in) ■ Autumn leaf pattern paper ■ Four gold-coloured leaf sequins/confetti shapes ■ Six gold-coloured turkey confetti shapes (leaves would also work)

COLLAGE

Collage can be a great way of using up bits and pieces you can't bring yourself to throw away but that aren't useful for much else. Whether cut out or torn, pieces of paper and card can be used together to create fabulous designs and patterns. You don't need a lot of equipment or expensive materials – you can just go ahead and have fun.

61 SNOW BUSINESS

Use scraps of paper in blending shades for fabulous backgrounds. Blues and white work well behind this chorus of colourful snowmen, dressed for the festivities. As long as it's colourful almost anything goes for this cheerful card. Have fun creating wacky patterned waistcoats, and see how many shades, patterns and textures you can get into the sky and the snow.

Store leftover papers by colour so you can easily find what you want for your next collage project.

■ White card blank 104 x 152mm (4 x 6in) ■ Scraps of paper in lots of colours ■ White card ■ Appropriate punches and stickers, if you have them ■ Seed beads in bright colours ■ Flower gems or paper flowers ■ Black pen

1 Cut a selection of blue and white papers into small pieces – the shapes can be as irregular as they come, as shown.

2 Arrange the pieces of paper to form a crazy patchwork on the card, with strong blues at the top fading to pale blues and whites along the bottom. Stick them down.

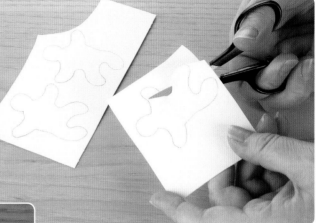

3 Trace the snowman template from page 106 and use it to cut three dancing snowmen from white card, reversing the template for one so that he is standing on his other leg.

4 Make a waistcoat for each snowman using the template on page 106 and remembering that one is facing the opposite way. Use various scraps of paper, punched shapes and so on for the decorations. Add beads as buttons and a buttonhole flower. Stick a waistcoat on to each snowman.

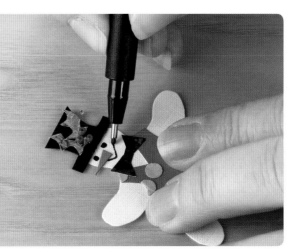

6 Draw faces on the snowmen with the black pen, add orange paper carrot noses and stick the snowmen on to the card using foam pads.

5 Cut out three black paper top hats, and decorate them with red beads and scraps of green paper to make holly sprigs. Stick them to the snowmen. Cut out a bow tie for each snowman and stick it on too.

Tear papers for collage instead of cutting **them for a softer finish.** Mulberry paper tears especially well, so it is used here for this patriotic 4th of July card. You could copy this idea for any flag, or use football colours for a boy's birthday card.

■ White card blank 144 x 144mm (5¾ x 5¾in) ■ Red card ■ White, red and blue mulberry paper ■ Two star-shaped white buttons ■ Four white buttons with red and blue stars on them ■ Red ribbon with a white trim ■ Narrow white ribbon ■ Small star punch

1 Tear a 12.5 x 10cm (5 x 4in) rectangle of blue mulberry paper and stick it to the front of the white card blank at an angle, referring to the photograph above as a guide.

2 Build up the rest of the flag using punched white mulberry paper stars (see step 5 on page 23) and 2cm (¾in) wide red strips. Trim the edges in line with the edge of the card.

3 Cut a piece of red card to fit the front of the card and cut an aperture in the centre 9cm (3½in) square. Edge the aperture with red ribbon. Tie narrow white ribbon into all the buttons and stick them on. Finally, stick the red frame to the front of the card.

Cover the whole surface of your pieces of paper with glue when making a collage to ensure a flat finish.

Recycle papers for your collage and save **waste.** This New Home card uses the lining side of old business envelopes to provide the colour, but you could get a unique effect from old wrapping paper, bags or paper scraps.

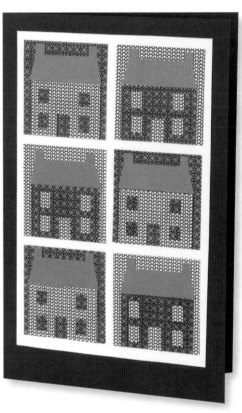

Iron old or used papers on a medium setting to get rid of any creases before you begin.

■ Dark blue card blank 104 x 152mm (4 x 6in) ■ White card ■ White business envelopes with different blue patterned insides (or scraps of blue patterned papers)

1 Trace the template from page 108 and use it to cut three houses from two envelopes and six roofs from a different envelope.

2 Cut three 4cm (1½in) squares from the first two envelopes. Stick each house centrally on a contrasting square. Stick on the roofs.

3 Cut rectangles for windows, matching their colour with that of the background and stick these on.

4 Cut a 9.5 x 14cm (3¾ x 5½in) rectangle of white card and arrange the houses on top, chequerboard style. Stick them in place then stick the white card centrally on the front of the card blank.

64 OUT OF AFRICA

Use collage for backgrounds, details, motifs, frames and more, creating a striking card for a man. Here a stunning paper mask is the centrepiece, embellished with paper-bead earrings and framed with matching colours.

- White card blank 144 x 144mm (5¾ x 5¾in)
- Mulberry paper in orange, beige and light brown
- Black paper and white paper ■ Zebra-stripe paper
- Colour pages from magazines, preferably glossy

1 Tear strips of mulberry paper and stick them randomly and vertically over the front of the card, overlapping them in places and leaving no white card showing. Trim the edges neatly as necessary.

2 Cut four 1.5cm (½in) strips of zebra-stripe paper, back them with white paper and stick them around the edges to form a border.

3 Cut four 1.5cm (½in) squares of black paper and stick them in the corners.

4 Trace the template from page 109 and cut out a black mask shape. Decorate it with white paper cut-outs, using the template as a guide. Stick the mask in the centre of the card.

Overlay transparent or semi-transparent papers to create new shades and colours.

6 With the pattern on the outside, roll up each triangle from the wide end, making the roll as tight as you can.

7 Glue the last 2.5cm (1in) or so of paper (towards the point of the triangle), using a cocktail stick or something similar to apply the glue. Press the end in place and hold until the glue starts to dry. Leave to dry completely, then stick in place on the card for the earrings.

8 Make four more beads from triangles 2.5cm (1in) wide at the base and stick them in the corners of the card to finish.

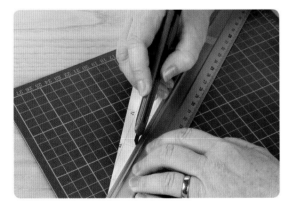

5 Cut four triangles from magazine pictures with a base 4cm (1½in) across and 20cm (8in) tall (the longer the triangle, the fatter the bead will be).

EYELETS AND BRADS

Colourful and versatile, eyelets and brads are pretty yet practical. They are great substitutes for glue sometimes, but they also look good in their own right. They can be plain and gloriously coloured or metallic, patterned or shaped and they come in increasingly varied sizes and designs. A few carefully chosen eyelets or brads can really give your cards a lift, as shown on these pages.

65 BABY FASHION

Use brads for decorative detailing – they add a great three-dimensional element. This baby card provides plenty of scope for experimenting. Have fun using brads as buttons or motifs on the tiniest baby clothes cut from pastel-coloured felt. You could use pinks or blues to make the card specifically for a boy or a girl or simply choose your favourites.

1 Cut a piece of patterned background paper to fit the card front exactly.

■ White card blank 144 x 144mm (5¾ x 5¾in)
■ Patterned background paper ■ Felt in pastel colours
■ Mini brads in various colours and patterns
■ Narrow baby ribbon and rickrack braid
■ White heart-shaped eyelets ■ Eyelet setting tools

Cut a small cross in the card with a craft knife or scalpel where you want each brad to go; this makes inserting it easy.

2 Trace the templates from page 109 and use them to cut clothes from felt (or draw your own designs). Decorate the clothes with brads, rickrack braid and ribbon, applying the trimmings carefully as in the examples, right. Make sure the arms of the brads don't show on the right side.

3 Position the clothes on the paper so that they form an attractive, balanced design using the photographs, left, as a guide. Stick them in place.

Use brads to represent buttons or poppers.

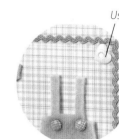

Use pretty eyelets rather than plain ones to turn a functional element into a decorative one.

Pick a shaped brad to represent the design on a T-shirt.

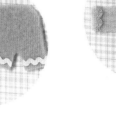

An extra piece of felt makes a hood and adds a touch of realism.

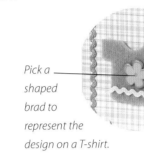

Look for very narrow trimmings like this baby rickrack braid, which looks in proportion.

4 Attach the paper to the card blank using a heart-shaped eyelet in each corner.

5 Stick a border of rickrack around the edge of the paper as a frame for the final touch.

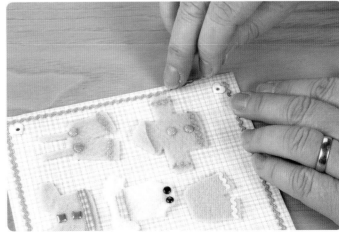

66 CHINESE FORTUNE

Attach vellum to paper or card without mess using eyelets (or brads). There's no need for glue and your card will be completed in no time. Bamboo is a Chinese symbol of good fortune, so it is most appropriate for this Good Luck card, which features three stamped Chinese messages of happiness, love and prosperity.

■ Dark green card blank 104 x 152mm (4 x 6in) ■ Dark green, white and orange card ■ Bamboo-patterned vellum ■ Orange eyelets ■ Eyelet setter ■ Small hole punch ■ Dark green ribbon 3mm ($^1/_8$in) wide ■ Feng Shui stamps: happiness, love and prosperity ■ Gold embossing powder ■ Embossing ink ■ Heat gun

1 Cut a 9 x 14cm (3½ x 5½in) rectangle of bamboo-patterned vellum and a rectangle of white card the same size. Place the vellum over the card and set orange eyelets in each corner to hold the layers together.

2 Cut a piece of orange card very slightly larger and stick the white card and vellum on top. Use a small hole punch to take out the orange card in the centre of the eyelets. Stick all three layers to the front of the green card blank.

3 Cut out a 5 x 9cm (2 x 3½in) rectangle of orange card. Mark 1.5cm (½in) from each top corner in both directions, then cut across each corner between the marks to make a tag.

4 Cut a piece of green card fractionally smaller than the orange tag all round and stick it centrally on to the tag. Set an orange eyelet at the top, as shown in the photograph above.

5 Use the embossing ink and gold embossing powder to stamp and emboss the Feng Shui symbols on the tag in the same way as for card 5 on page 11.

6 Cut a narrow strip of bamboo patterned vellum and stick it to a strip of white card the same size. Attach it across the tag with two orange eyelets. Trim off any excess.

7 Finally, tie a double length of narrow green ribbon through the eyelet at the top of the tag and attach the tag to the card using sticky foam pads.

Eyelets don't have to be round any more – they are available in an increasing number of novelty shapes. Look out for shapes that enhance your theme.

67 LOVELY LUGGAGE

For a great farewell card, select eyelets for their unashamedly lovely looks. You can mix different designs and sizes to work well with charms and trimmings.

- Cream card blank 144 x 144mm (5¾ x 5¾in) ■ Striped paper, brown paper and pink paper ■ Tiny pink eyelets 3mm (⅛in) ■ Pink and white floral eyelets ■ Ribbon charm ■ Handbag charm ■ Eyelet setting tools

1 Mark off the bottom 10cm (4in) of the card front in pencil. Cut a piece of striped paper to fit and stick it in place.

2 Draw a curved handle in the centre of the top section and cover it with brown paper. Cut around the handle, leaving it attached at the bottom. Trim the card back level with the top of the bag.

3 Cut four triangles of brown paper and stick them over the corners of the striped paper, rounding them slightly. Position and set the tiny pink eyelets on the handle and on the corner triangles.

4 Cut a narrow strip of brown paper and slide the ribbon charm on to it for the strap. Stick it in place. Attach the other charm to the suitcase with a strip of brown paper.

5 Make a pink tag 5 x 3.5cm (2 x 1½in) and mount it on a larger brown tag. Add your greeting and apply the flower eyelets. Attach the tag to the suitcase with a narrow strip of brown paper.

When you are using a lot of eyelets that are basically decorative, it is easier to set them in place on a shape before attaching it to the card.

68 RING OUT THE ROMANCE

Use eyelets to 'draw' simple yet eye-catching designs. Use plain eyelets for the main outline and fancy eyelets for decoration. It's a simple technique but great fun, and you can experiment with a range of designs. These bells are superb for announcing a wedding.

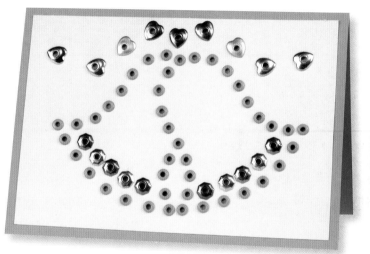

Mark the position of eyelets with pencil before you begin to avoid making a mistake.

- Pale blue card blank 104 x 152mm (4 x 6in) ■ Ivory textured card ■ Round, pastel-coloured eyelets ■ Heart-shaped eyelets in pastel metallic colours ■ Octagonal eyelets in pastel metallic colours ■ Eyelet setting tools

1 Cut a rectangle of ivory card slightly smaller than the card blank. Trace the bell template from page 110 and transfer it to the back of the ivory card.

2 Punch holes about 1cm (½in) apart along the outline of the bells and set round, pastel-coloured eyelets into these holes.

3 Draw a curving line outwards from where the bells join at the top, and set heart-shaped eyelets at intervals along the line.

4 Set octagonal eyelets across the bells as decoration, just above the lower edge of each bell.

5 Stick the ivory card centrally on to the blue card blank, covering the backs of the eyelets.

DIE CUTS

A die-cutting machine enables you to cut shapes from paper, card, foil or even fabric to embellish your cards quickly and professionally, and it makes light work of repeat shapes, especially when you are making cards in bulk, as at Christmas. There are hundreds of designs to choose from, and because you can change what you cut them from, the shapes look different every time. Shapes can also be bought ready cut.

69 GHOSTLY GLOW

(23) Use die cuts as masks, dusting chalk over them to create shadowy outlines. The idea is perfect for these ghostly forms designed to terrify at Halloween. Here one white ghost hovers above the surface on foam pads for added impact.

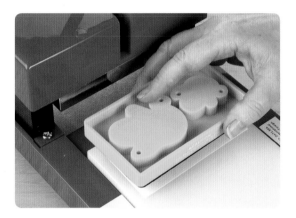

1 Place you ghost die rubber side down over white paper on the cutting mat of the cutting machine.

■ Black card blank 100 x 210mm (4 x 8¼in) ■ Ghost die and cutter or ready-cut ghost shapes ■ White paper ■ Repositionable adhesive ■ Very pale blue or grey chalk ■ Chalk applicator or cotton wool

2 Push the plate and die into the machine under the pressure plate and pull the handle down, as shown. Release the handle, remove the die and plate from the machine and then remove the cut shapes. Punch six small ghosts and one large one in this way.

3 Using a very small amount of repositionable adhesive, stick a row of six small ghosts along the black card blank.

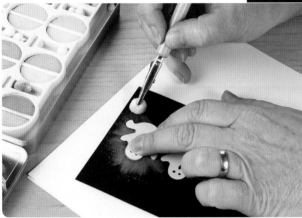

4 Using a chalk applicator or cotton-wool ball sweep the chalk over the ghosts, working outwards from the centre on to the black card, as shown. Now dab the chalk over the eyes and mouths, making sure it gets on to the card underneath.

Ensure that your die cuts are completely flat when dusting over them – hold them down well with your fingers.

5 Lift the paper ghosts off the card to leave only the shadowy silhouettes.

6 Stick the larger ghost in place over the silhouettes using sticky foam pads to raise it off the surface so that it appears to float.

70 POP-UP FLOWERS

Use die-cuts to make simple pop-ups to give the recipient of your card a delightful birthday surprise. The flowers here pop-up inside a fan-shaped card and more flowers provide a colourful pattern on the front. Outlining the flowers with black ink adds a delightful hand-drawn look and accentuates the shapes of the die cuts.

■ Pale blue pearlescent card blank with a scalloped edge, or cut your own scallops on a 144 x 144mm (5¾ x 5¾in) card ■ 125 x 125mm (5 x 5in) paper in red and in cream ■ 14 x 1.5cm (5½ x ¾in) strip of white card ■ Black pen ■ Flower on stem die and cutting machine

1 Die-cut two cream and four red flowers, referring to the technique for card 69 on pages 74–75. Trim the stems on two red and one white flower, using the photograph above right as a guide. Outline the die-cut flowers using the black pen.

2 Fan the three long-stemmed flowers on the front of the card with stalks crossing at the lower left-hand side. Stick them in place.

3 Measure 2cm (¾in) from each end of the strip of white card and score and fold it backwards. Make a second fold 2cm (¾in) beyond the first fold at one end.

4 Stick the single-fold end of the card strip to the inside front of the card blank from the centre fold, 2.5cm (1in) above the bottom of the card (see the open card above).

5 Apply glue to the other end up to the first fold, fold the strip back at the second fold and close the card blank carefully, so that the glued part sticks to the other half of the card blank.

6 Open the card and the strip should stand out, ready for you to attach the die-cut flowers.

7 Stick the three short-stemmed flowers on to the front of the card strip, again in a fan shape with the white flower on top.

Die-cut paper upside down to create a reverse image.

You don't have to make the pop-up section if time is short. This card looks good even without the surprise inside.

71 SMALL PACKAGES

Use repeated die-cut shapes in different colours for a simple but effective design.
They say that the best gifts come in small packages, so here are ten for the lucky recipient.

- Orange card blank 100 x 210mm (4 x 8¼in)
- Coloured papers in dark blue, red, orange, pale blue, turquoise and lemon
- Gifts die and cutting machine (or ready-cut parcel shapes)

Pick a textured paper to make plain die-cuts look a little more interesting.

1 Use the die to cut out two small parcels and bows in every colour except dark blue.

2 Stick a bow on to each parcel as shown on the card above.

3 Cut a rectangle of dark blue paper slightly smaller than the card blank.

4 Stick the parcels on the blue paper in two vertical rows. Stick the paper on to the card blank.

72 STARRY, STARRY NIGHT

Hang die-cut shapes inside apertures to add movement. Decorate your die-cuts with beads, sequins and glitter for added embellishment.

Cut extra die cuts to make coordinating gift tags.

- Purple card blank 104 x 152mm (4 x 6in)
- White card
- Gold glitter
- Beads and sequins
- Star-shaped die and cutting machine
- Circle cutter
- PVA glue
- Narrow adhesive tape

1 Die-cut seven large and two tiny stars in white card. Cover them with PVA glue and decorate them with beads and sequins. Before the glue dries sprinkle glitter over them.

2 Unfold the card. Lightly mark a central vertical line on each panel in pencil. Score and then fold along each line, folding the edges in to the middle. Draw around a curve (a plate or something similar will do) to create the archway at the top and cut along the lines.

3 Cut two 3.5cm (1¼in) circular apertures and one 1.25cm (½in) circular aperture in each flap. Stick three stars down the centre of the card and hang stars in each aperture with narrow tape.

These two crafts work very well together, and are often used on the same project. Both are easy and require very little specialist equipment. Although designs are produced especially for the crafts it is very easy to adapt patterns from other sources and you can introduce other crafts such as stamping for a modern look.

73   EASTER ELEGANCE

Prick a design on to parchment in the traditional way for a card of great delicacy. The narcissi design used here make the most of the parchment's tendency to whiten where it has been pressed, and is complemented by elegant pricked borders around each corner flower. The yellow of the card blank adds colour and gives this Easter card a fresh, spring feel.

■ Yellow card blank 104 x 152mm (4 x 6in) ■ Parchment paper 208 x 15mm (8 x 6in) ■ White gel pen ■ Fine embossing tool or stylus ■ Paper pricking tool ■ Soft surface such as craft foam ■ Narrow yellow ribbon – at least 70cm (28in) long ■ Rounded corner punch (optional)

1 Trace the narcissus template from page 107. Fold the parchment in half to make it the size of the card. Open it out and centre the inside left-hand side (the front of the card) over the narcissus design. Trace over the lines of the template using the white pen. Include the lines of the pricked border.

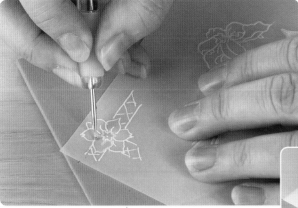

2 Using the fine embossing tool and with a medium-soft surface such as craft foam beneath the parchment, draw around the lines of the design. Press down enough to emboss the paper but not tear it.

3 Using the embossing tool, rub gently on the flower petals to whiten and shade them at the centres and at the tips of the petals, as shown.

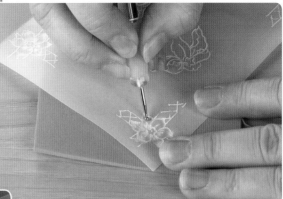

4 Using the paper-pricking tool, prick holes along the lines of the borders in the corners. Use a ruler to keep your lines straight. Turn the paper back to the right side and round off the right-hand corners with scissors or a corner punch.

If you don't have a pricking tool, use a strong sharp needle with its eye end embedded in a cork.

5 Open out the card blank and apply a line of glue to the back, right next to the fold. Centre the parchment over the card and press in place so that the back half of the parchment paper is attached to the card.

6 Stick a length of narrow yellow ribbon down the inside centre fold of the card, leaving a tail of at least 20cm (8in) at top and bottom. Tie the tails together in a bow at the front of the card. Trim the ends as necessary.

74 GOLDEN KOI

Use pricking to add detail to card shapes.
It's a bit like embossing, and a far cry from traditional pricked designs, giving your work a modern twist. These koi stand out against deep blue water and appear to move elegantly through the ripples. This card suits many occasions and would particularly appeal to a man, though you may not want to give it away!

- White card blank 100 x 210mm (4 x 8¼in)
- Paper in plain colours for the fish and water in orange, yellow, dark blue, mid-blue and turquoise ■ Pricking tool and surface to work on such as craft foam
- Blue pen to mark in the eyes

1 Trace the koi fish template from page 108 on to the back of the orange paper; trace two more on to the back of the yellow paper with the design reversed on one of the fish.

2 Working on a slightly soft surface such as craft foam, prick along the lines of the fish outlines and details to capture the scaly texture of the fish.

3 Cut around the outside of the fish shapes, taking care not to cut into the pricked holes. Ideally use small, sharp scissors for this so you can follow the graceful curves as closely as possible.

4 Cut a rectangle of dark blue card to fit the front of the card blank. Arrange the fish on to the blue card, referring to the card, right, for positioning and then stick them in place. Trim the tails of the top and bottom fish as necessary to fit the card.

5 Cut curving ripple shapes from mid blue and turquoise paper following the lines of the fish and stick them around the fish shapes, again referring to the card here as a guide.

6 Finally mark the eyes on the fish with blue pen to bring your fish to life.

Use a careful dusting of chalk to accentuate detail pricked on to pale colours.

75 BUNNY FOR BABY

Create softly tinted images on parchment by colouring on the back. The pastel colours created are ideal for a christening card, as here, but could work equally well for many other occasions.

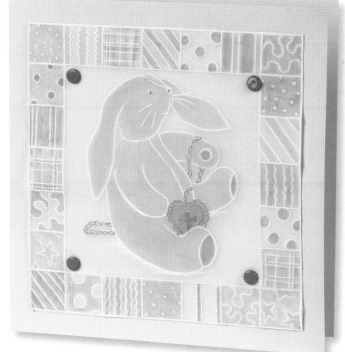

When using coloured pencils on the back of parchment, begin by making the pencil marks quite faint and build up colour if you need to – it is easy to add more colour but hard to take it away.

■ Square cream card blank 144 x 144mm (5¾ x 5¾in) ■ A5 piece of parchment paper ■ White paper or card ■ Small embossing tool or stylus ■ Coloured pencils in a selection of colours ■ White and gold gel pens ■ Vellum tape or glue ■ Closed eyelets in mauve ■ Eyelet setting tools

1 Trace the rabbit design from page 110. Lay the parchment on top and trace over the design lines with white pen. Draw over the white ink with the embossing tool, resting on a surface with a slight give in it, such as craft foam (see step 2 on page 79).

2 Now for the fun part – colour in the back of the picture (the side you drew on) using coloured pencils.

3 Trim the edges of the picture and mount it on white paper or card, using vellum tape or glue around the edges. Trim the card around the edges of the vellum and add the eyelets. Mount the panel on the card blank and highlight the locket and chain with gold pen.

76 CHRISTMAS IN THE ROUND

Prick patterns around delicate parchment motifs to give a decorative edge. Gold pen, drawn over some of the embossing, provides a lovely accent on this festive card.

Use only a minimum of glue on the back of parchment and allow it to dry partially before sticking the parchment down.

■ Deep red card blank 69 x 184mm (2¾ x 7¼in) ■ Green holographic paper ■ Scraps of parchment ■ Embossing tool ■ White and gold gel pens ■ Pricking tool ■ Narrow ribbon ■ Circle cutter

1 Using the templates on page 108, trace and emboss the motifs on to parchment. Emboss a 2.5cm (1in) circle around each motif. Highlight parts of each motif using the gold pen on the raised side.

2 Prick holes close together in zigzags around the edge of the circles, making lots of little points. Run the pricking tool gently over the holes to break them, leaving a fancy edge around the circles.

3 Stick lines of ribbon down each side of the card. Cut a 3cm (1¼in) circle of holographic paper to back each motif and stick the parchment circles in place on the ribbon lines.

TEABAG FOLDING

Also known as kaleidoscope folding, teabag folding creates amazing patterns from tiny squares of paper. There are now lots of specialist papers available for folding, or you can create your own, as long as each square has an identical pattern. Put together, the origami-based shapes create even more patterns. Even using plain paper the designs are stunning. Here one folding pattern is used in four different ways.

77 'TIS THE SEASON

Make pretty rosettes for a festive feel. They look great on this Christmas card or you could use just one for a birthday rosette. These are made from squares of wrapping paper and plain gold paper, though you could use specialist tea-bag paper. Ribbon stripes give the background pattern and depth without detracting from the folded shapes to complete this eye-catching effect.

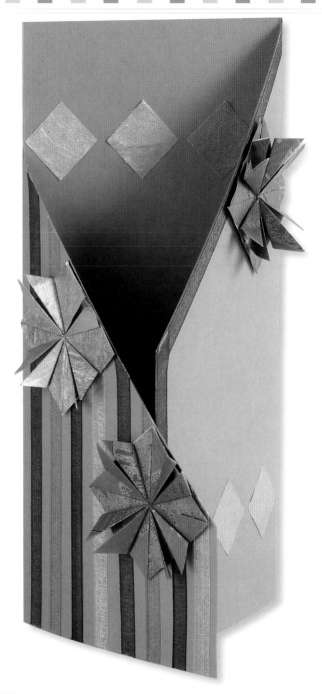

- A4 sheet of green card
- Gold paper ■ Christmas paper with a repeat pattern
- Scrap card ■ Sheer ribbons in red, green and gold
- Circle cutter or 2.5cm (1in) diameter round punch

1 Cut out four identically patterned 5cm (2in) squares of gold paper for each rosette. Fold one piece of paper from corner to corner with the right side up. Open it and fold it from corner to corner using the opposite corners. Open it out.

2 Fold the paper in half horizontally. Open it out again. You have made three mountain folds on this paper.

When using patterned paper make sure you cut each square with the pattern in exactly the same place and begin folding with the same section of pattern facing you.

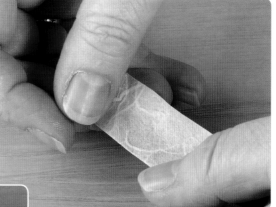

3 Turn the paper over and fold it in half lengthways, where there is no fold, wrong sides out. This creates a valley fold on the right side.

4 Open out the paper again and turn it to the right side. Push the valley fold in and flatten the paper to form a triangle, as shown here.

5 Fold the top corners in to the centre to make a point, as shown. Make four identical shapes.

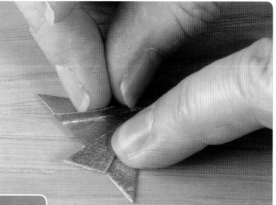

6 Cut a 2.5cm (1in) circle of scrap card and stick the folded shapes on top to form a rosette. Make two more rosettes using the Christmas paper in the same way then complete the card following the guidelines overleaf.

Make the basic card by scoring and folding the card into three equal sections.

Cut 2.5cm (1in) gold paper squares and stick them diagonally across the centre panel and lower edge of the right-hand panel to echo the shapes of the rosettes.

Position the rosettes so they overlap the edges of the card and trim them to fit.

Edge the right-hand panel with more ribbon.

Decorate the left-hand panel with sheer coloured ribbons applied as stripes.

Trim the front edges of the card diagonally to shape the card.

78 DANCING BUTTERFLIES

Use teabag folding to create pretty butterfly motifs. These exotic golden butterflies look as if they are about to take flight. The vellum chosen for the wings captures the delicacy of these creatures.

- Cream card blank 69 x 184mm (2¾ x 7¼in)
- Gold vellum and floral vellum
- Gold three-dimensional paint
- Gold gel pen

Rub the folded edges with a bone folder for a crisp finish.

1 Cut a 2.5cm (1in) wide strip of floral vellum and a slightly wider strip of gold vellum. Stick the floral strip on top of the gold one then stick them both on the card blank.

2 Cut and fold ten 2.5cm (1in) gold vellum squares as explained on pages 82–83, steps 1–5. Pair them up, points together, to form butterfly shapes and stick them on the card.

3 Use three-dimensional gold paint to create the heads and bodies. Finally, draw on the antennae using the gold gel pen.

79 STAMPED SENSATION

Make your own teabag papers using stamps. It's fun and easy to do and opens up a huge range of possibilities. Here, an embossed silver pattern gives a rich feel to a birthday card.

1 Stamp four pink squares on white paper using the square ink stamp then stamp and emboss four silver square patterns on top (see page 11). Cut them out and fold them as for card 77.

2 Cut a square of pink vellum to fit the card front and stamp and emboss four silver square patterns in the centre. Stick the vellum to the card blank around the edge of the silver squares.

3 Cut twenty 4cm (1½in) squares of pink paper and fold them as before. Arrange them to create a frame around the silver squares and stick them down. Stick deep pink ribbon on the central square to make a diamond then stick the rosette in the centre.

If you have one, use a clear quilter's ruler to cut perfect squares of paper every time.

■ White card blank 144 x 144mm (5¾ x 5¾in) ■ Pink vellum ■ White paper and plain or slightly patterned pink paper ■ Deep pink ribbon ■ 4cm (1½in) square pattern rubber stamp ■ 2.5cm (1in) pink square ink stamp, or foam square and pink ink ■ Embossing ink ■ Silver embossing powder ■ Heat tool

To keep the points of your folded papers flat, use a tiny amount of glue underneath the folds.

■ Cream card blank 104 x 152mm (4 x 6in) ■ Pale blue, yellow and orange papers ■ Patterned papers in five colours ■ Blue felt-tip pen

80 LET'S FLY A KITE

Use teabag folding to create a fabulous kite design. Fold plain and patterned papers and put them together to make the kite with a fluttering multi-coloured tail. Children will love how the unusual shape of the card shows off the kite and allows it to 'fly'.

1 Cut from the top of the centre fold to the bottom corners of the card blank to create a triangle. Cut a piece of pale blue paper to fit the card front and stick it in place.

2 Cut three 5cm (2in) squares of yellow paper and two orange squares the same size. Fold two squares of each colour as explained on page 83; stick the points down. Glue the folded shapes on the remaining paper square to form the kite.

3 Stick the kite at the top of the card, overlapping the edge. Draw a line snaking down from it using the felt-tip pen.

4 Cut two identical 2.5cm (1in) squares of each of the patterned papers. Fold them and place them together at intervals along the line.

STICKERS AND PEEL-OFFS

Stickers are great for card making. They are very easy to use, need no special equipment and take up very little storage space. There is a sticker for every occasion and for every type of card. You can combine different stickers, layer them for a three-dimensional effect and even embellish them for a more ornate effect. They can be used in so many ways or combined with other techniques for even more possibilities.

81 CROCUS FOR MOTHER

Layer pretty stickers using foam pads for a three-dimensional delight. You only need two versions of the sticker(s). Flowers always work well with this treatment, like the crocus on this Mother's Day card. Frame it with a soft pastel colour and place it on a delicate vellum background for a very feminine and modern card that picks up on a seasonal theme.

■ Cream card blank 104 x 152mm (4 x 6in) ■ Mauve metallic corrugated paper ■ Patterned vellum ■ Cream card ■ Two identical crocus stickers ■ Mauve and silver square brads

1 Carefully cut the crocus out of its background and stick it on to cream card. Trim around it neatly.

Cut out stickers and arrange them to your satisfaction before pulling them off their backing paper and sticking them in place because mistakes are difficult to rectify.

2 Arrange leaves from both sticker sheets on a 6 x 10cm (2¼ x 4in) rectangle of cream card, as shown. Check they will look good with the crocus placed over them. Stick them in place.

3 Stick the crocus over the top using sticky foam pads to raise it off the surface.

4 Cut a 7 x 11.5cm (2¾ x 4½in) frame from the corrugated paper with an 8.2 x 4.5cm (3¼ x 1¾in) aperture in the centre. Stick it centrally over the crocus design, as shown. Fix silver square brads in each corner of the frame at an angle as diamond shapes.

5 Cut a piece of patterned vellum a little smaller than the card blank and stick the centre of it to the front of the card.

6 Stick the framed crocus to the centre of the card, over the vellum. Finally, attach the vellum in the corners with square purple brads as diamond shapes.

82 Luck of the Irish

Create impact by echoing the shapes of your stickers on card mats. This shamrock is the perfect design for a St Patrick's Day card. The green shamrock stickers may be simple, but, when added to layers of green card repeating their shapes, they look brilliant and have great impact.

■ White card blank 100 x 100mm (4 x 4in)
■ Three shades of green paper ■ Shamrock stickers

Rub over stickers gently to ensure that they are properly stuck down.

1 Stick the stickers on to pale green paper and, using the stickers as a guide, draw the outline of a larger shamrock on the paper.

2 Cut around that outline, stick the shape on to medium green paper and repeat the process. Repeat again on dark green for the largest sticker only.

3 Cut a square of pale green paper to fit the card blank. Stick the largest shape in the top left-hand corner then stick the other three curving around it as shown in the photograph.

4 Finally, stick the green square on to the front of the card blank to complete your card.

83 Dragonfly Days

Use clear stickers over punched shapes or rub-ons for a glossy look. The stickers draw attention to what's under them – in this case the number of a special birthday and punched dragonflies.

■ Bright turquoise card blank 69 x 184mm (2¾ x 7¼in) ■ Patterned blue and green paper ■ Plain green paper ■ Black rub-on numbers ■ Transparent bubble stickers, 2cm (¾in) and 2.5cm (1in) square ■ Dragonfly punch

Cut motifs from magazines or wrapping paper and use them like stickers, simply gluing them in place.

1 Rub the number 21 three times on to green paper. Stick the smaller stickers over the numbers and cut round them.

2 Punch two dragonflies from patterned paper and stick them on green paper. Stick the larger stickers on top and cut round them.

3 Cut five 7cm (2¾in) x 1.5cm (½in) strips of patterned paper and stick them across the card at intervals. Trim as needed. Attach the stickers over the patterned strips to complete this clever card.

84 BIRTHDAY BAND

Use glass paints to colour in black peel-offs on acetate for a glowing stained-glass effect. Cut and combine peel-offs as you wish and place them in apertures to show them off. The bright colours make this a very appealing child's card, but with different designs and colours you could make this card suitable for an adult or teenager.

1 Cut four circular apertures in the front of the yellow card, three 2.5cm (1in) in diameter down the right-hand side, and one 4.5cm (2¾in) in diameter on the left.

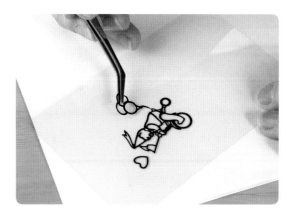

2 Lift the peel-offs away from the backing sheet and place them on the acetate. If you use the same peel-offs as shown here, cut off the balloons and add them to the back of the tricycle, as shown.

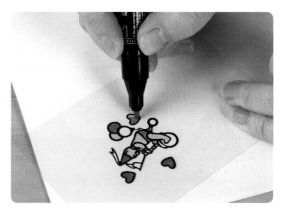

3 Paint carefully within the lines of the peel-offs. The pens shown make this easy. Allow the paint to dry and add a second coat, if necessary.

4 Stick the acetate in place behind the apertures so that the designs are centred nicely.

5 Back the acetate with a piece of white paper cut to fit the back of the card front and add the musical note peel-offs to the front to finish.

- Yellow card blank 100 x 100mm (4 x 4in)
- Black peel-offs ■ White paper ■ Circle cutter
- Glass/ceramic paint pens in red, yellow and blue
- Circle cutter

Use a craft knife to cut and move peel-offs.

POLYMER CLAY

Polymer clay is a great modelling material that gives you the opportunity to make your own decorations for cards. It comes in fabulous colours, is easy to use, and can be hardened easily without special equipment. You can use it in all sorts of ways.

85 SCROLL OF HONOUR

Press ordinary objects into clay to leave decorative impressions. In this case a brass button created the pattern on the red seal. The bright three-dimensional stars suggest success and an exciting future for the graduate who will receive this card.

■ Dark blue card blank 104 x 152mm (4 x 6in) ■ Red and yellow clay ■ Cream paper ■ Brass button with raised crest or pattern ■ Star cutter 2cm (¾in) high ■ Ivory pearl rub-on wax ■ Red

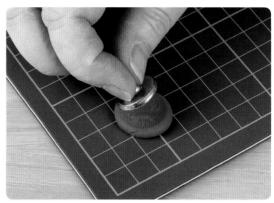

To prevent items sticking to clay when you are using them to make impressions, coat them with a little cooking oil first.

1 Roll a small ball of red clay, roughly 2cm (¾in) in diameter and flatten it slightly. Press the button into it then remove the button to create the look of a seal.

2 Roll out some yellow clay and use the cutter to cut seven 2cm (¾in) stars. Bake the clay items, if necessary, or allow them to dry naturally, following the manufacturer's instructions.

3 Roll up a piece of cream paper 10cm (4in) wide to make the scroll. (The length doesn't matter.)

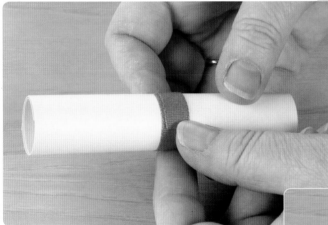

4 Wrap a piece of ribbon around the roll and stick the end down to secure the roll.

5 Add tails of ribbon and stick the seal on to them.

6 Rub the stars with ivory pearl wax and then stick them and the scroll on to the blue card.

86 ON THE ROAD

Use clay to make your own buttons – they are great embellishments. Here they are used for the wheels of some funky little cars for a fun card to celebrate a driving test pass.

To give clay buttons a really professional look roll with a rolling pin or a smooth cylinder of some sort to give a very flat surface.

■ Black card blank 100 x 210mm (4 x 8¼in) ■ Polymer clay ■ White thread ■ Cocktail stick or similar ■ 2cm (¾in) round cutter ■ Patterned papers, black paper and pink paper

1 Roll out little clay and cut out two circles for each car. Make two holes in the centre of each circle with a cocktail stick to create a button. Make sure the holes open at the back as well. Bake the clay or leave it to dry naturally, following the manufacturer's instructions. Tie white thread through each one.

2 Trace the template from page 110 and use it to cut four cars from patterned paper. Stick the cars on black paper and trim around each one, leaving a very narrow black outline.

3 Stick the cars down the middle of a 20 x 9cm (7¾ x 3½in) rectangle of pink paper and stick on the wheels. Now stick the pink paper to the front of the card blank.

87 RUBY WEDDING

Impress clay with a rubber stamp to make ornate panels. The panels work well combined with stamped panels that have been embossed, giving positive and negative images of the same design.

To give clay the texture of something soft, such as fabric, wrap the material round a rolling pin and then press it on the clay.

■ White card blank 104 x 152mm (4 x 6in) ■ Pink patterned paper ■ Card in pale pink and red ■ Red polymer clay ■ Rubber stamp and red inkpad ■ Clear embossing powder ■ Heat tool ■ Red gemstones

1 Roll out red clay about 3mm (⅛in) thick and press the rubber stamp into it. Cut around the stamped area to make a panel 4cm (1½in) square. Make two more. Make a dip in the centre of each panel for the gemstones. Bake the shapes or allow them to dry naturally, following the manufacturer's instructions.

2 Stamp and emboss three images on the pink card. Cut them 4cm (1½in) square. Mount the squares on red card and trim around the panels, leaving a narrow border. Cover the front of the card with pink patterned paper then stick the red card on top. Finally, glue a red gem in the centre of each panel.

THREE LITTLE DUCKS

Use shrink plastic instead of polymer clay to make cute embellishments. Just cut out the shapes, heat them in the oven and, when cool, paint them up. These yellow ducks are placed on a bib shape for a baby card and smaller ducks line up along the bottom.

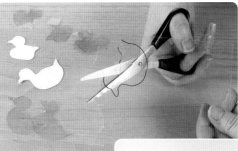

1 Using the templates on page 108, trace the duck motifs and transfer three large ducks and five small ducks on to shrink plastic. Cut out the shapes.

2 Heat them following the manufacturer's instructions – this doesn't take long. Sometimes it helps to put a sheet of paper over them to keep them flat but when they cool they should flatten anyway.

3 Leave them to cool then paint them with yellow acrylic paint, as shown.

Cut just inside the drawn lines when cutting out the shrink plastic shapes to avoid picking up the colour of the pen.

- Pale green card blank 104 x 152mm (4 x 6in)
- Yellow card and white card ■ Patterned paper
- Shrink plastic ■ Yellow ribbon 3mm (¹⁄₈in) wide
- Pale green ribbon 1cm (³⁄₈in) wide
- Yellow acrylic paint

4 Cut a piece of patterned paper slightly smaller than the card front and stick it in place.

5 Using the template from page 108 cut out the yellow back of the bib and the white front from card. Stick the white piece on to the yellow one and stick the bib on to the card.

6 Make two small bows from yellow ribbon and stick them at the top of the bib, using the photograph above left as a guide.

7 Stick a length of green ribbon across the bottom of the card, about 2.5cm (1in) from the bottom edge, and stick five small ducks along it using sticky foam pads.

8 Use sticky foam pads to stick the three larger ducks to the bib, raising them off the surface like the smaller ducks.

STENCILS

Stencils are fun to use and a great way to be creative without the need to draw. With a little imagination, you can use a single stencil in many ways for a different look each time, so they give great scope for working out your own designs. Stencils can be used with lots of materials, including paint, ink, pens and pencils. Designs vary from very simple and modern to ornate and traditional with lots in between. You can even make your own.

89 FROM LEAF TO PETAL

Use one simple shape to make a whole design. Here it creates both leaves and petals. Stencil overlapping leaf shapes on dark green card, adding a few pink petals for a semi-abstract background. Then put six pink shapes together to make a separate flower and add a gold centre to set it off perfectly. What a wonderful multi-purpose card this is.

■ Pink card blank 100 x 210mm (4 x 8¼in) ■ Green card and white card ■ Acetate sheet ■ Acrylic paints in pink, white, three shades of green and gold ■ Sponge (a washing-up sponge is fine) ■ Circle punch 1.5cm (½in) in diameter (optional)

1 Draw round two curves to create a leaf template approximately 4cm (1½in) long.

2 Use this template to cut out a leaf stencil from the acetate sheet with a craft knife. Keep the acetate shape you cut out to use as a mask.

3 Cut a rectangle of green card to fit the front of the pink card blank. Using the stencil, sponge random leaf shapes on to this with the green paints. To do this, hold the stencil in place and dab a piece of sponge lightly covered in paint down on to the stencil until the whole shape is coloured.

4 Add some pink petals at the edges, masking the rest of the card with scrap paper. Use the acetate leaf shape to mask some shapes to create leaves pointing out from underneath. When the paint is dry, trim the green card, making it fractionally smaller than the pink card blank. Stick it centrally on the pink card to leave a narrow pink border all round.

Avoid overloading the sponge with paint – you can build up the colour with several layers if need be and avoid mess.

5 Stencil six pink shapes in a circle on the white card, all meeting at the centre. Mix some white paint with the pink and stencil this paler colour lightly over the pink shapes.

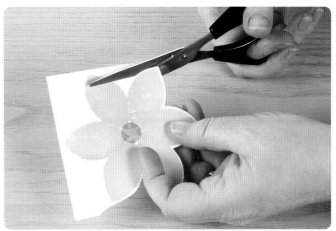

6 Punch or cut a 1.5cm (½in) circle from a piece of scrap card and use this as a stencil to sponge a gold circle in the centre of the flower. Cut out the pink flower, leaving a very small border of white card around the edges of the petals then stick this at the top of the card to finish.

90 HERE COMES THE SUN

Choose one delightful stencil as your main motif then use elements of it to make a border. This is really easy, and if you choose your stencil carefully it works so well. This cheerful sunflower motif stencilled in bright colours has great charm and would please either a child or adult.

■ Blue card blank 104 x 152mm (4 x 6in) ■ Dark blue card ■ Sunflower stencil ■ Dark yellow, green and burnt orange acrylic paint ■ Sponge ■ Rounded corner punch

Remember to check that paint from one layer has dried thoroughly before putting a stencil back on to use a second colour.

1 Sponge the flowers from the stencil on to dark blue card with yellow paint. Transfer a small flower repeatedly around the edge of the blue card blank in the same colour.

2 Once dry, use green paint to add stalks and leaves to the main design and border. Stencil over the yellow centres of the flowers in burnt orange. Do this lightly so that some yellow shows through.

3 Trim the dark blue card to 12.5 x 6.5cm (5 x 2½in), with the design centred. Round off the corners. Using yellow paint roughly sponge the edges of the dark blue paper and the blue card.

4 Stick the dark blue panel in the centre of the card using foam pads to raise it off the surface.

91 BIRTHDAY BUNCH

Draw round your stencil motif with a pen then colour in the design for a hand-drawn look. Choose some pretty coloured pencils to colour in the design and add a few additional embellishments.

■ Deep yellow card blank 100 x 100mm (4 x 4in) ■ Floral bouquet stencil ■ Cream card ■ Gold vellum ■ Shimmering ribbon in brown and orange, 6mm (¼in) wide ■ Fine-nib brown pen ■ Coloured pencils in green and deep and pale yellow

Turn a stencil over to get variety in the way flowers, leaves and other elements point.

1 Place your stencil on cream card and carefully draw round the shapes with a fine brown pen. Colour in the flowers and leaves with coloured pencils then cut out the shape.

2 Cut a 6.5cm (2½in) square of gold vellum. Stick the bouquet in one corner and wrap the side corners across to the centre over it. Stick the edges of the vellum in place.

3 Make a small bow with the two shades of ribbon and stick it to the front of the vellum. Stick the bouquet diagonally across the front of the card using the photograph as a guide.

4 Use the stencil to draw flowers and leaves in the top left and bottom right corners of the card blank. Colour in the flowers and the leaves to finish, making these flowers pale yellow.

92 SNOW ROMANCE

Apply three-dimensional paint using a stencil for a whole new look. Add pink glittery hearts and snowflakes to the figures of the snow people to capture the shimmer and sparkle of the season. Kids will love this technique so you could create Christmas cards like this working together as a family.

■ Pale blue card blank 104 x 152mm (4 x 6in) ■ Turquoise card
■ Snow people stencil with snowflakes ■ Three-dimensional
paint in gold, green and white ■ Acrylic paint in pink and white
Pink glitter ■ Tube of silver three-dimensional paint
■ Heart punch

Place three-dimensional paint on the stencil at one side then swipe it across smoothly in one go for a smooth finish.

1 Swipe three-dimensional white paint across the snowflakes stencil with a plastic spreader or a piece of card to make a border of snowflakes around the edges of the pale blue card. You will need to allow some to dry before completing the border.

2 Cut a 7 x 11cm (2¾ x 4¼in) rectangle of turquoise card. Punch a heart shape in a scrap of card and use the card as a stencil apply white three-dimensional hearts tinged with pink acrylic paint. Sprinkle glitter on to the hearts before the paint dries.

3 Masking off any parts of the stencil not required, use the gold, green and white paints to complete the picture on the turquoise card, as shown right. Add snowflakes using dots of silver three-dimensional paint.

4 Use white acrylic paint to add snow at the bottom of the turquoise card and to colour the edges. Stick the turquoise card to the blue card using foam pads.

METAL

Available as sheets, ready-made shapes or as fine leaf, metal can be used to decorate cards in a variety of ways and many metal products have been produced specifically for crafters to use. Although particularly suitable for anniversaries or weddings, metal's wonderful properties makes it a lovely addition to almost any card. Most metals require strong adhesive and you may need one or two cutting tools.

93 LINGERING LOVE

Emboss silver sheets with patterns and combine with beads on silver wire for a luxury look. Icy blue beads and flowered paper complement silver sheet metal and wire and are perfect for a 25th anniversary card.

- White card blank 104 x 152mm (4 x 6in) ■ Silver coloured metal sheet ■ Blue floral patterned paper ■ Embossing tool (optional) ■ Soft surface such as craft foam ■ Hole punch ■ Silver wire ■ Blue and silver beads

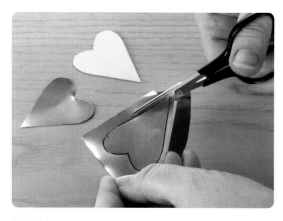

1 Draw a heart shape on the metal sheet and cut it out. Cut another slightly larger heart. You may find it helpful to draw the hearts on paper first and make templates to draw around.

2 Place the smaller heart on a soft surface, such as craft foam, and use the embossing tool (or a sharp pencil) to draw squiggles all over the heart.

If you are uncertain about embossing freehand, use a tracing and draw over it, then go over the lines again to emboss them properly.

3 Turn the heart over and stick it centrally on the larger heart. Punch one hole at the top and three at the bottom.

4 Cut a 7cm (2¾in) square of metal sheet and emboss the edges as before. Cut a 6cm (2³/₈in) square of patterned paper and stick it in the centre, as shown. Stick this square to the card diagonally to make a diamond shape.

5 Make a tiny loop at the end of a piece of wire and thread approximately 2.5cm (1in) of beads on to it. Push the straight end through a hole at the bottom of the heart, bend it over and twist the end around the top of the beads; trim off the excess. Do this twice more in the other two holes.

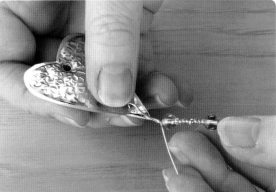

6 Pass a piece of silver wire through the top hole in the heart, twist the ends together and feed a bead on to them. Punch a hole in the card and push the ends of wire through the card to fasten the heart in place. Stick the ends of wire to the back and cover them with a piece of card to finish.

94 LUCKY HORSESHOES

Use a punch to cut metal sheets for super-shiny motifs. Here, silver horseshoes have been combined with striped paper horseshoes for luck and to create a simple but effective design.

■ White card blank 69 x 184mm (2¾ x 7¼in) ■ Mauve card ■ Small horseshoe punch ■ Brightly coloured striped paper ■ Silver-coloured metal sheet ■ Self-adhesive silver-coloured metal sheet ■ Black pen

Use plain sheet metal for punching (and sharpening your punches) but for flat areas use self-adhesive metal sheets for speed.

1 Punch out five silver horseshoes and five striped horseshoes. Now cut out five 3.5cm (1¼in) self-adhesive silver squares and five striped squares the same size. Cut mauve card to fit the card blank.

2 Stick a 0.5cm (¼in) strip of silver sheet across the top and bottom of the card and stick the silver and striped squares alternately down the card. Stick a silver horseshoe on each striped square and a striped horseshoe on each silver one. Use the black pen to mark nails on the horseshoes.

95 POTTY ABOUT PLANTS

Embellish a card with metal tags for a gardening theme. Here metal and paper tags decorate a couple of pots for an unusual and light-hearted card suitable for many occasions.

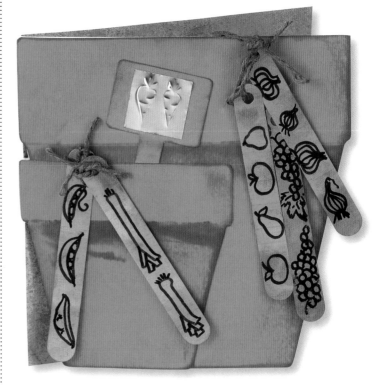

■ White card blank 144 x 144mm (5¾ x 5¾in) ■ Terracotta and brown paper ■ Green patterned or textured paper (or use a green card blank) ■ Copper-coloured garden tags ■ Dusting chalks ■ Silver-coloured metal sheet ■ Black indelible marker pen ■ Garden twine ■ Fine embossing tool and soft surface to work on such as craft foam

1 Draw simple flowerpot shapes and cut two pots from terracotta paper. Dust on dark brown chalk for shadows.

2 Cut out the label from brown paper with a smaller piece of metal sheet to go on top. Emboss carrots into the back of the metal and stick it to the paper label. Draw fruits and vegetables on the copper tags using black pen. Tie lengths of twine in the holes at the end.

3 Stick the terracotta pots and tags to the front of the card. Cut green paper to fit the card and stick it to the inside. Finally, cut around the terracotta pots where they are not touching the edges of the card to reveal the green inside.

If you don't have a fine embossing tool, a ballpoint pen will do just as well, as any ink will be on the back and not show.

96 KEY TO THE DOOR

Use metal flakes to transform simple card shapes. The technique is perfect when you want to create a very special effect, as here, where the keys and numbers look wonderful against a background of tiny stars.

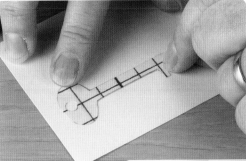

1 Trace the key templates from page 109 and use them to cut the keys out of double-sided adhesive sheet. Stick each key on to cream card.

2 Remove the backing sheet from the shapes and place small amounts of metal flakes over the top, rubbing them gently to attach and smooth down the metal pieces.

3 Rub and clean away the excess from the edges of the shapes, and give the shapes a final rub with your finger to polish the metal. Cut out the keys.

4 Cut out the number 21 from double-sided adhesive sheet, and cut a fob shape from teal card. Stick the number on the card fob and cover it with metal flake as before. Pass wire through the holes in the keys and curl it round to make a key ring.

5 Stick star sequins all over the front of the card. Stick the keys, fanned out, at the bottom of the card using foam pads then stick the key fob at the top over the key ring using the foam pads as before to raise it off the surface.

■ Teal greeting card blank 104 x 152mm (4 x 6in) ■ Scraps of light teal and cream card Double-sided adhesive tape ■ Metal flakes ■ Gold-coloured wire ■ Star sequins

Use a soft eraser to clean away excess metal from the edges.

QUILLING

Quilling is a craft that was popular with the Victorians and is experiencing a revival of popularity in the 21st century. Modern colours and designs can create cards that are just right for our time but utilize the same skills. Although quilling looks very complex and detailed, it doesn't take long to master the skill of winding the paper strips tightly then letting them relax and forming them into teardrops, ovals and curls that will give full rein to the imagination.

97 KING OF THE JUNGLE

Combine quilled shapes with card ones for representational images. To make a cute children's birthday card, curl brown paper to suggest the flowing locks of the magnificent mane and create leaf shapes for the eyes.

■ Cream card blank
144 x 144mm (5¾ x 5¾in)
■ A4 sheets of paper in
three shades of brown
■ Cream paper and
patterned corrugated paper
■ PVA glue ■ Quilling tool
■ Black pen

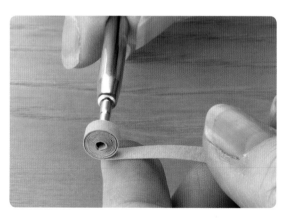

1 Cut two 31 x 0.3cm (12 x ⅛in) strips of the palest brown paper, plus 12–15 strips of dark brown and 15–20 strips of mid-brown. Slipping one end of the first pale brown strip into the notch at the end of the quilling tool, wrap the strip round and round the tool tightly.

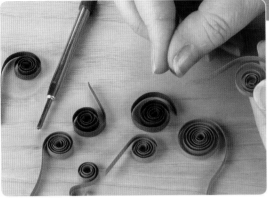

2 Remove the paper from the tool and allow it to open a little between your fingers to form a circle approximately 2cm (¾in) in diameter. Using a tiny dab of PVA glue on a cocktail stick, glue the end of the paper in place. Once the glue is dry pinch one side of the circle between your finger and thumb to create a teardrop shape. Make a second shape. These are the ears.

Hold the rolls closed for longer before releasing them for tighter curls.

3 Using the mid and dark brown papers, make a number of loose circles, some with ends stuck in place, others with ends left to curl away. Use the complete length of paper for some; use half the paper or less for others to give a variety of sizes.

To create the face, stick the smaller cream circles on to the largest circle. Colour a scrap of cream card with black pen, cut out a small triangle and add it to make the nose.

Let the ends of paper curls spiral around other circles for a flowing look.

4 For the face cut a 5.5cm (2¼in) diameter circle from the palest brown paper and three 2cm (¾in) diameter circles from scraps of cream paper. For the feet cut two 2.5cm (1in) diameter circles from pale brown paper. Draw on the claws and cut wisps of paper for the whiskers, as shown above. For the eyes, pinch two mid-brown coils at both ends to make leaf shapes. Arrange the features on the face (see above and right).

5 Stick the lion's ears to the card using the face as a guide to positioning (but don't stick the face on yet). Stick the curls in position around the lion's ears, with the dark brown at the top of his head and the mid brown down the sides and under his chin. Stick the face and paws over the curls, and add a border cut from corrugated paper to finish.

Use black pen to draw the claws on the feet. To raise them up add a few extra quilled circles underneath.

Cut short, very thin lengths of brown paper and stick them to the face for whiskers.

98 Spot the Flowers

Easy-to-make quilled flowers make great decorations for your cards. The pink quilled whorls of the border complement the flowers and the spotty paper that brings the card bang up to date.

■ White card blank 100 x 210mm (4 x 8¼in) ■ Dark, bright and pale pink paper ■ Brown spotted paper ■ Quilling tool ■ Circle cutter

Try quilling with patterned paper for an additional design element.

1 Cut 13 strips of bright pink paper 21cm (8¼in) long and 3mm (⅛in) wide for the border quilling. For each flower cut an 18 x 1.5cm (7 x ½in) strip of paper – cut two pale pink, two dark pink and three bright pink strips. Make cuts along the edge to fringe it.

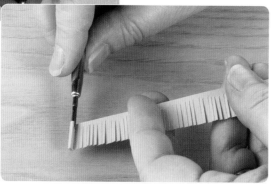

2 Position the quilling tool at the end of the uncut edge of each flower strip, as shown, and roll the paper tightly.

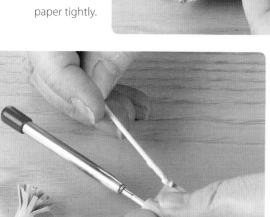

4 Cut a 7.5cm (3in) diameter circular aperture above the centre of the white card blank as in the photograph above.

5 Cut a piece of spotted paper to fit the card front and cut an identical aperture in that. (Place the paper over the card and draw round the aperture lightly in pencil to help with positioning.) Stick the paper to the card.

6 Use the thin strips of bright pink paper to wind whorls, winding half the strip one way around the quilling tool and then winding the other end in the opposite direction. Loosen the coils to form a neat S-shape.

7 Stick the whorls around the circular aperture and across the card near the bottom between two narrow strips of pink paper.

3 Stick the unfringed end down and remove the quilling too. Open out the 'petals' to form the flower.

99 AROUND AND AROUND

Make simple quilled circles and arrange them in a geometrical pattern for a great card for a man. The secret is in the colours, so match at least one colour to your background, as shown.

■ Card blank 100 x 100cm (4 x 4in) ■ Paper in three colours or shades ■ Quilling tool

1 Cut your paper into strips 21cm (8¼in) long and 3mm (⅛in) wide. Make 25 quilled circles by rolling the paper tightly using the quilling tool. Let each roll relax between your fingers to form a circle approximately 1.5cm (½in) in diameter; stick the end of the paper in place.

2 Arrange the circles in a pattern on the front of the card blank and stick them in position. Use the photograph as a guide or your own geometrical design.

Use a cocktail stick to place tiny amounts of glue on the bottom of the circles to stick them down.

100 FASHIONISTA'S FAVOURITE

■ Blue card blank 104 x 152mm (4 x 6in) ■ Gold, floral and deep turquoise papers ■ Quilling tool ■ Small gemstones ■ Circle cutter ■ Gold gel pen

Make fun fashion accessories from quilled circles and teardrops for a glamour girl. Place the accessories on circles of patterned paper surrounded by gold for a thoroughly feminine look.

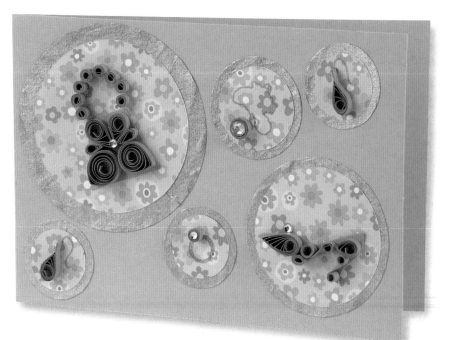

1 Draw small shoe and bag templates on scrap paper and use them to cut a bag and a shoe from turquoise paper. Cut some strips of paper 3mm (⅛in) wide. Quill a selection of circles and teardrops in varying sizes. Fit them on to the shapes and stick them down.

2 Stick the shapes to circles of patterned paper and add tight circles to make a handle for the bag. Add a gem to the centre of the bag and to the top of the shoe.

3 Cut smaller circles of patterned paper and quill teardrops for the earrings and tight circles for the ring and necklace. Stick them in place. Complete these designs using the gold pen and gemstones.

4 Cut a set of gold paper circles slightly larger than the patterned paper circles and stick the patterned paper circles on top. Stick the circles to the card.

Vary the size of your quilled shapes by using different lengths of paper, as well as by how loose you make the shapes.

TEMPLATES

Here are the templates you'll need to complete the projects in this book. They are exactly the size required so simply trace them and transfer them as required.

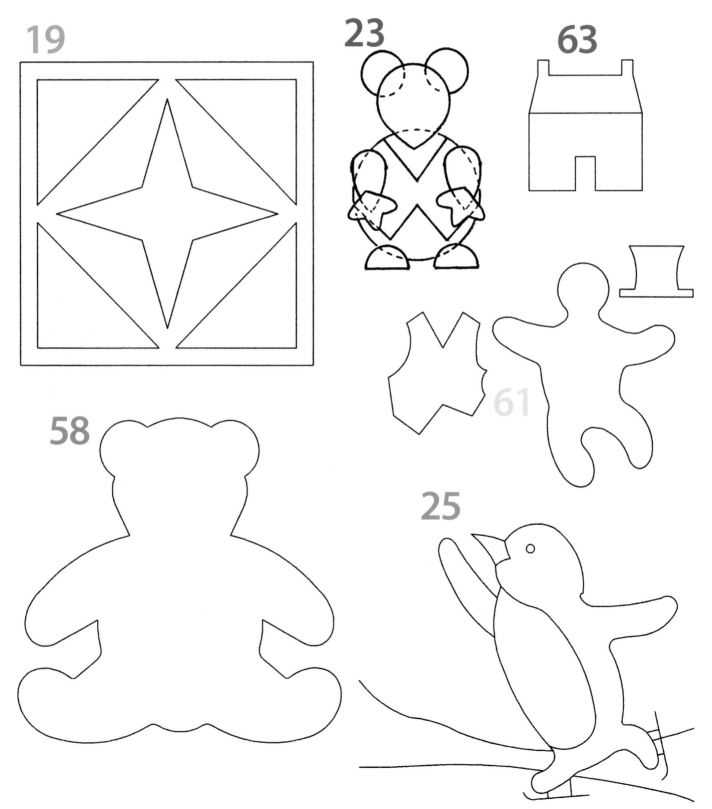

19

23

63

58

61

25

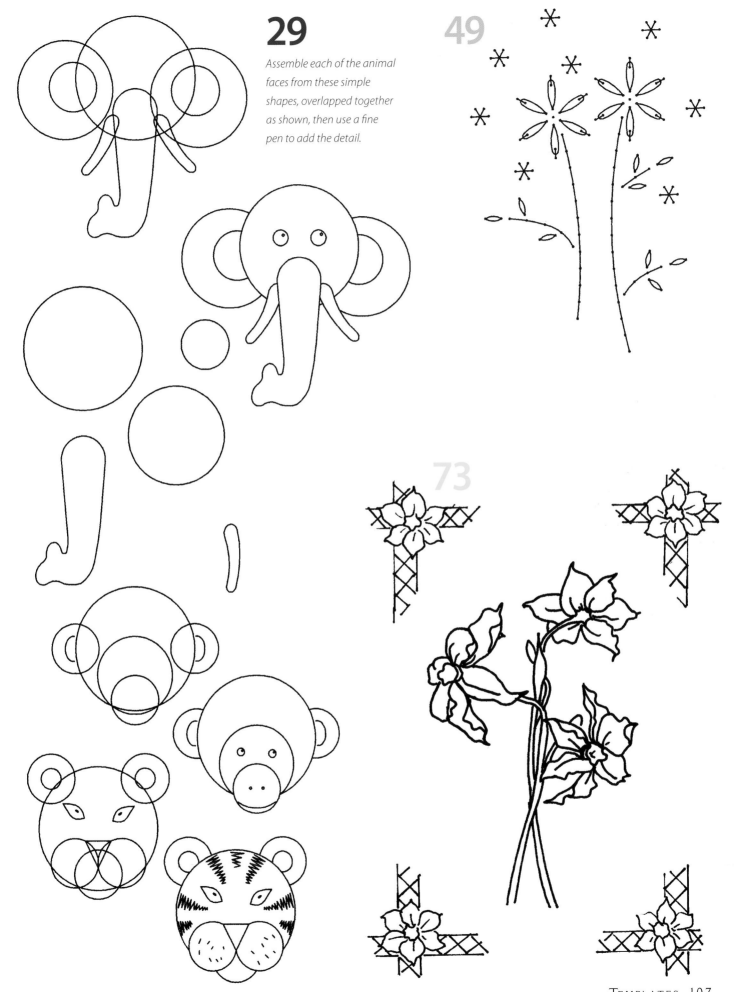

29

Assemble each of the animal faces from these simple shapes, overlapped together as shown, then use a fine pen to add the detail.

49

73

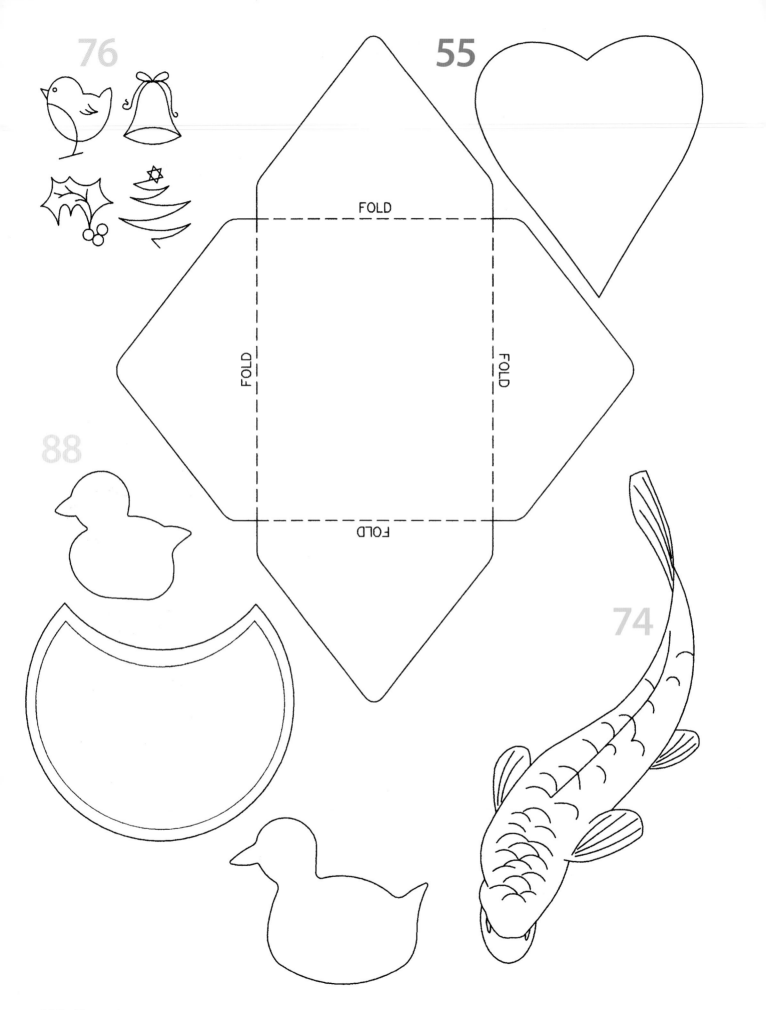

76

55

FOLD

FOLD

FOLD

FOLD

88

74

64

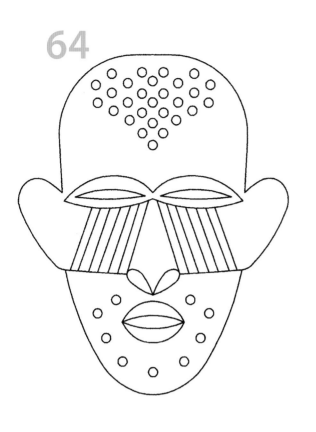

96

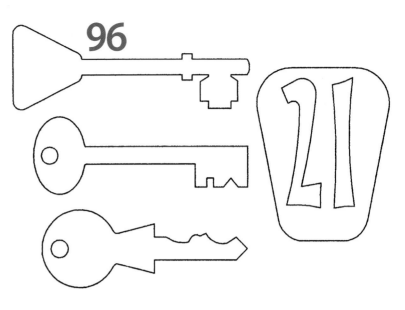

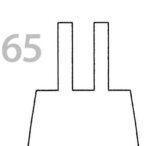

65

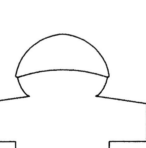

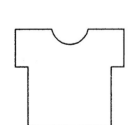

53

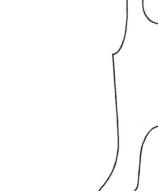

75

36

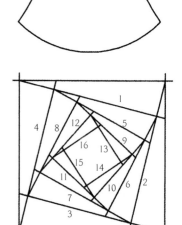

50

68

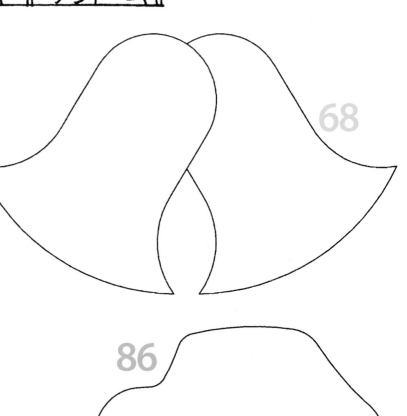

86

SUPPLIERS

Nearly all the card blanks used this book were provided by Craft Creations. Visit their website at www.craftcreations.com or telephone on 01992 781900.

Other products came from the following suppliers:

1 Butterfly stamp from Stamps Happen (Butterflies 90247)

2 Background stamp from Stamps Happen; flower Dimension Fourth

3 Easter egg stamp from Stamps Happen (Decorated eggs 90386)

4 Mortarboard stamp from Amuse Artstamps (Grad Cap 2 –7025C)

5 Teen girl stamps from Woodware Craft Collection (Girl Talk FRCL022)

9 Baby stencils from All Night Media Inc. (Plaid 46505)

10 Shapeboss stencil from Fiskars (Swirl)

11 Tag stencil from Marianne Design (EL4204)

12 Wedding cake stencil from Lasting Impressions (L516)

16 Feet embellishments from Dress It Up (Baby)

47 Edge punch from Fiskars (Heart)

48 Paddle punches from Sizzix (Swirl 38-0830, Hand 38-0840)

54 Liquid Pearls from Ranger

55 African pattern corrugated paper by Creativity International

61 Leaf punch Woodware Craft Collection (2135); flower punch by E K Success

69 Ghost die Sizzix (38-0252)

65–68 Eyelets and brads supplied by ArtCards

66 Rubber Stamp from Lakeland Limited (2030 2450)

70 Flower die Sizzix (38-0928)

71 Parcel die Sizzix (38-0152)

72 Star die Sizzix (hearts, stars and tag Sizzlet)

78 Floral vellum by CR Gibson (Timeless Romance)

81 Crocus Stickers from Mrs Grossman

82 Shamrock stickers from Mrs Grossman

83 Rub-ons from Creativity International

84 Teddy peel-offs from Craft Creations; Vitrea 160 pens from Pebeo

90 Sunflower stencil from StenSource International

91 Floral stencil from U.I.T. (Daffodil 11602/1021)

92 Snowpeople from Darice Inc.; 3D paint from Heritage Handcrafts

94 Horseshoe punch by X-Cut; self-adhesive sheet metal from Shortcuts TM www.shortcutscrafts.com

STOCKISTS

Paints

Pebeo Inc, *305 Avenue de Bertagne, BP 106, 13881 Gemenos Cedex, France, products available from craft stores, www.pebeo.com*

Stamping

A Muse Artstamps, *6537 Palatine Avenue North, Seattle, WA 98103 USA, tel: 1-877-783-4882.*

All Night Media Inc. *Norcross CA 30091-7600 USA, available from craft stores*

Dimension Fourth Ltd, *86 Rotherham Road, Barnsley, South Yorkshire S71 1UL UK; tel: 01226 213627 or go to www.dimensionfourthltd.com*

Stamps Happen Inc. *part of* **Janlynn**, *available from craft stores or visit www.stampshappen.com*

Woodware Craft Collection *in the UK; tel: 01756 700024*

Stencils

Diane Dorward, *27 Hawkwood Close, Malvern, Worcestershire WR14 1QU, UK; tel 01684 564056 or visit www.dianedorwardcrafts.com*

Heritage Handcrafts, *Littleton CO 80163 USA; available from craft stores*

General card-making supplies

ArtCards *16 Noel Coward Close, Burnham on Sea, Somerset TA8 1QE, UK, tel: 01278 784627 or go to www.artcards.co.uk*

Craft Creations Ltd, *Ingersoll House, Delamare Road Cheshunt, Hertfordshire EN8 9HD, UK; tel: 01992 781900 or go to www.craftcreations.co.uk*

Creativity International, *Narrowboat Way, Hurst Business Park, Brierley Hill, West Midlands DY5 1UF; tel: 01384 485550 or go to www.cilimited.co.uk*

Darice Inc. *Strongsville OH 44149 USA, available from craft stores*

Fiskars UK Ltd, *Newlands Avenue, Bridgend, Mid Glamorgan CF31 2XA; tel: 01656 655595 or visit www.fiskars.com*

Gregory Knopp, *products direct from www.gregory-knopp.co.uk*

Janlynn, *C R Gibson, Memories in the Making, stockist details from SoloCraft: www.solocraft.com*

Lakeland Ltd, *Alexandra Buildings, Windermere, Cumbria LA23 1BQ, UK. Stores nationwide; tel: 015394 88100 or go to www.lakeland.co.uk*

Lasting Impressions, *Woods Cross, Utah USA, products available from craft stores or buy from www.lastingimpressions.com*

Letraset Ltd, *Kingsnorth Industrial Estate, Wotton Road, Ashford, Kent, TN23 6FL; tel: 01233 624421 or go to www.letraset.com*

Ranger, *Union Falls NJ 07724*

Royal & Langnickel, *products available from craft stores; tel: 01384 258188 in the UK or 800-247-2211 in the USA; www.royalbrush.com*

Simply Create, *Stowe-on-the-Wold; tel: 01451 833547*

ACKNOWLEDGMENTS

I would like to thank Alicia at Simply Create, Bridget at Clear Communications, Helen at Lakeland Limited, Jonathan at Creativity International, Kim at Craft Creations, Melissa at Sizzix, and Sonia at SoloCrafts for all their help while I was creating the cards for this book. I'd also like to thank my husband Jim, my mother, Jenny Dixon, and Cheryl Brown at David and Charles for their support and encouragement. Also my thanks go to all family friends and colleagues who had to put up with my bad memory and lack of time for them.

INDEX

achievements
   driving test 92, 110
   graduation 9, 90–1
   sporting 37
adhesives 5
animals 28, 30, 34–5, 37, 102–3
anniversaries
   flower fancy 60
   gold 42–3
   punched hearts 52
   ruby 92
   silver 21, 98–9
aperture cards 4

baby cards 21, 56, 70–1, 93, 108, 109
   birth 14–15, 64, 106
   christening 81, 110
beads 26–9, 36, 37, 98
birthdays
   see also children; men
   18th 48
   21st 88, 101, 109
   birthday bunch 96
   dragonfly days 88
   fashionista's favourite 105
   in the frame 25
   garden harvest 45
   for the love of flowers 8
   old-world charm 16
   parcel post 29
   perfect party 49
   pop-up flowers 76
   putting on the glitz 10–11
   stamped sensation 85
bon voyage 18–19, 20, 58, 73
boys, birthday 12, 68, 85
brads 70–3, 111
brass-rubbing technique 33
butterflies 6–8, 84

card 4, 5, 111

celebrations
   4th of July 68
   Easter 9, 40, 44, 78–9, 107
   Halloween 56, 74–5,110
   Mother's Day 6–8, 33, 86–7
   St Patrick's Day 88
   Thanksgiving 65
   Valentine's Day 61, 62–3, 108
children's birthdays
   all hands on deck 53
   animal magic 34–5, 107
   birthday band 89
   bobbing balloons 12
   brown mouse 28, 106
   fairy ring 49
   king of the jungle 102–3
   let's fly a kite 85
   rocket racer 12
   simple spirelli 57
Christmas
   family portrait 44
   jingle bells 41, 110
   mosaic masterpiece 44
   in the round 81, 108
   snow business 66–7, 106
   snow romance 97
   star of wonder 24, 106
   starry night 77
   super skater 30–2, 106
   'tis the season 82–4
   tree star 65
collage 66–9
confetti 62–5
congratulations see achievements
crayons 30–3

die cuts 74–7, 111
driving test 92, 110

Easter cards 9, 40, 44, 78–9, 107
edges, decorative 4
embossed cards 4, 40
embossing
   heat 10–13
   paper 14–17
engagement 28, 73
equipment 5
eyelets 70–3, 111

fabric painting 30–1
fish 13, 58, 80, 108, 109
flowers
   anniversaries 60
   birthday 8, 25, 76, 96
   Easter 44, 78–9, 107
   greetings 22–4, 40, 46–7, 52, 54, 94–5, 96, 104
   Mother's Day 33, 86–7
folding card 5
Fourth of July 68

gardeners 44, 45, 100
get well cards 22
girls, birthday 10, 105
glue 5
good luck
   Chinese fortune 72
   harlequin 16
   lucky horseshoes 100
   new home 38–9, 68, 106
   new job 18–19, 26–7
   retirement 18–19
graduation 9, 90–1
greetings cards
   dancing butterflies 84
   flower dimensions 52
   flowers of the field 24
   from leaf to petal 94–5
   hearts and flowers 22–3
   here comes the sun 96
   lovely in lavender 40

magic circles 46–7
   proud peacock 37
   sew easy 54–5, 107
   soft and simple 33
   spot the flowers 98, 104
   swirling leaves 50–1

Halloween 56, 74–5, 110
harvest 44, 45
heat embossing 10–13

Iris folding 41, 110

kaleidoscope folding 82–5

leaving card 18–19

men
   around and around 105
   fishing 13
   golden koi 80, 108
   mists of time 32
   ocean waves 58–9, 109
   out of Africa 69, 109
   potty about plants 100
   sheer abstract 61
   small packages 77
metal 98–101
Mother's Day 33, 86–7
mulberry paper 22–5

new home 38–9, 68, 106

paints 30–3, 111
paper embossing 14–17
paper folding 82–5
parchment craft 78–81
peel-offs 86–9, 111
pencils 30–3
photographs 18, 42–5
polymer clay 90–3
pop-up flowers 76
pricking 78–81
punches 50–3, 111

quilling 102–5

retirement card 18–19
ribbon 38–41
romance see anniversaries
rubber stamps 6–9, 25, 85, 111
rub-ons 46–9, 111

St Patrick's Day 88
sewing 54–6
spirelli 57
sporting achievements 37
stencils 14–17, 94–7, 111
stickers 65, 86–9, 111
suppliers 111

tags 18–21
teabag folding 82–5
Thanksgiving 65
threads and fibres 54–7, 64
tools 5

Valentine's Day 61, 62–3, 108
vellum 58–61

weddings
   see also anniversaries
   absolutely charming 36
   dream cake 17
   from the heart 28
   ring out the romance 73, 110
wire 34–7
work-related 18–19, 26–7